GenMar

Generational Marketing Strategy

Basket to Casket Marketing 101

By David Selley

i

Other Books by David Selley:

- *PAPA #1: The Boy in England and Growing Up Tough*
- *PAPA #2: The Young Man in Canada*
- *PAPA #3: The Businessman and Entrepreneur in the USA*
- *PAPA #4: The Entrepreneur (Papa Secrets)*
- *PAPA #6: MARRIED – The Four Seasons of Marriage*

Additional books and series by David Selley are forthcoming. See page 128 for the latest titles.

Publisher: Promptings Publishing
Fran Jessee has dedicated her expertise to editing and formatting David Selley's works, ensuring his authentic voice, entrepreneurial wisdom, and marketing insights are preserved for readers worldwide. For publishing inquiries, contact fran@franjessee.com

Cover Design: David Selley
ISBN 979-8-9916760-8-3
Printed in the United States of America

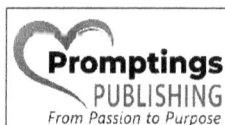

Promptings
PUBLISHING
From Passion to Purpose

May You Have

Enough happiness to keep you *sweet,*

Enough trials to keep you *strong,*

Enough sorrow to keep you *human,*

Enough hope to keep you *happy,*

Enough failure to keep you *humble,*

Enough success to keep you *eager,*

Enough friends to give you *comfort,*

Enough wealth to meet your *needs,*

Enough enthusiasm to look *forward,*

Enough faith to banish *depression,*

Enough determination to make each day

better than *yesterday.*

(Author Unknown)

Aloha! From beautiful Hawaii!

David Selley

Dedication

To every entrepreneur, executive, and brand builder bold enough to think beyond the sale — and build something that truly resonates across generations.

And to those who never stopped believing in the power of **marketing with meaning**.

— *David Selley*

Disclaimer

The information contained in this book is based on publicly available sources, personal experiences, and professional observations. While every effort has been made to ensure the accuracy and reliability of the content, the author and publisher make no guarantees and assume no responsibility for errors or omissions.

Any references to specific companies, brands, or individuals are included solely to illustrate marketing strategies, generational trends, or business outcomes. These references do not constitute endorsements, criticisms, or formal evaluations of those entities. The inclusion of such examples is intended for educational and illustrative purposes only.

All trademarks, product names, and company names or logos cited herein are the property of their respective owners and are used strictly for informational purposes. Readers are encouraged to conduct their own research and make independent business decisions.

Foreword

As the publisher of this work, I've had the distinct privilege of working closely with David Selley to bring this ground-breaking book to life.

What you hold in your hands is not just another business book.

It's a deeply personal and powerful roadmap—built from decades of real-world experience, earned wisdom, and strategic insight.

David's understanding of marketing reaches far beyond tactics and trends. His insights come not from theory, but from time spent on the front lines of global cosmetics—watching the rise and fall of brands based on how well (or how poorly) they connected with the generations they served.

This book delivers what so many entrepreneurs, executives, and brand builders are missing: A lens for thinking generationally.

It's not just about reaching your audience—it's about remaining meaningful to them over time.

The GenMar Strategy outlined in these pages isn't a trend. It's a shift in how we communicate, connect, and earn trust across generations.

It has been my honor to help bring this message to the world.
— *Publisher*

PREFACE

Why This Book, Why Now

"Your story is your legacy—let it inspire the world."
— *David Selley*

We live in a world obsessed with speed—where branding often chases the next viral moment instead of building for the next generation. In the rush to be noticed, many businesses overlook the most valuable opportunity of all: creating something that lasts.

This book is about Generational Marketing—the art of shaping a brand that evolves with your customer and stays relevant over time. *This book isn't just meant to inspire you — it's designed to guide you. You'll learn how to identify generational gaps, apply practical strategies, and reshape your business to earn loyalty that lasts.* It's a call to shift your focus from today's sale to tomorrow's loyalty, and to ask a more enduring question: *What will they remember about you 20 years from now?*

I'm David Selley. I spent 27 years in the global cosmetics industry—starting on the pavement with Revlon, later working with brands like Lancôme, and eventually stepping into executive roles where I had a front-row seat to the rise (and fall) of some of the most iconic names in beauty. What made the difference? Not the product—but how well the brand adapted to the changing values of the generations they served.

After that chapter, in my business career I continued as an entrepreneur—launching ventures, advising companies, and learning the same lesson across multiple industries:

generational awareness is one of the most valuable tools a business can have.

This book is filled with real stories and relevant case studies— lessons learned from the front lines. Some are from my own ventures. Others come from the brands I observed up close. All of them reveal patterns and decisions that shaped customer loyalty — or lost it.

While many of the stories begin in cosmetics, the insights go far beyond. Whether you're a coach, a consultant, a retailer, or a business leader, the message remains the same: the brands that stay meaningful are the ones that grow with their customers.

Inside, you'll find practical tools, reflection points, and a clear framework I call the *GenMar Strategy*—a straightforward approach to understanding, reaching, and resonating with your audience across generations.

You'll hear my voice and my stories. But more importantly, I hope you begin to see your own business. Because whether you're selling lipstick or leadership, this isn't just about your product—it's about your people. And people evolve.

That's the heart of generational marketing—building trust that endures, not just attention that fades.

— *David Selley*

About the Author

David Selley is a lifelong entrepreneur, strategist, and story-teller whose journey began not in a boardroom, but as a bold 15-year-old who ran away from home in England to forge his own path. Even before that, he had the instincts of a businessman—buying and reselling stamps, sharpening his skills with every risk he took.

Those early lessons carried him across three countries and into a remarkable 27-year career in the global cosmetics industry, where he worked with legendary brands like Revlon and Lancôme. His deep understanding of marketing, product positioning, and customer behavior was shaped not only by strategy but by real-time shifts in generational trust and consumer trends.

In his 60+ years of entrepreneurship and business, David has built and advised multiple companies through moments of reinvention, expansion, and meaningful growth. His insights come not from theory—but from the trenches.

Now at 87, he is actively pursuing a Guinness World Record as the oldest author to publish the most books in a single year. His *Papa Series of Memoirs*, including *Papa the Entrepreneur* and *The Businessman in the USA*, capture the ventures, values, and personal stories that have defined his life's work.

David is also the founder of the **International Entrepreneurs Association (IEA)**, a global platform dedicated to empowering new generations of entrepreneurs through mentorship, legacy thinking, and global connection. As part of this mission, he created the **Famous 50 Legacy Book** series—featuring curated collections of high-achieving professionals across industries, each sharing their story, expertise, and impact in a beautifully published legacy volume. These collaborative books not only spotlight excellence, but also provide entrepreneurs a way to preserve and promote their influence for future generations.

This book is one part of that mission—a strategic blueprint designed to help brands speak across generations, earn trust that lasts, and stay relevant in a world that never stops changing. See page 162 for a full list of David Selley's Book Series.

Who This Book Is For

Whether you're a solo entrepreneur, a startup founder, or the CEO of a legacy brand, this book was written with you in mind. Inside, you'll find practical tools and timeless insights—whether you're building a loyal audience from the ground up or leading a company through the challenges of generational shifts.

The GenMar Strategy adapts to you—because relevance isn't about team size. It's about mindset.

For leaders at every level—
solopreneurs to enterprise teams—
this is the blueprint for building a brand that lasts.

How to Use This Book

A Guide for Entrepreneurs, Small Teams and Legacy Leaders

This isn't a book you simply read once and shelve. It's a strategy, a reference, and a step-by-step how-to guide you'll return to as your business evolves. Whether you're:

- A solo entrepreneur building a personal brand
- A consultant or creative shaping loyalty through story
- A leadership team member guiding a multi-generational company into the future

...the GenMar Strategy was designed to scale with you.

How to Get the Most Out of It:

• Start with the chapters that speak to your current challenges—branding, leadership, messaging, or emotional loyalty.

• Follow the case studies and "Ask Yourself This" prompts to apply the insights to your business in real time.

• Use the Strategy section at the end of the book to start putting GenMar into action—it includes reflection prompts and practical frameworks for solo builders and teams.

A full GenMar Toolkit with additional tools and templates is coming soon. Join the waitlist at GenMarStrategyTools.com *to be first to know when it's available.*

You don't have to follow this book in perfect order. Let it meet you where you are—and return to it as you grow. This isn't just a book. It's a reference manual for relevance, trust, and legacy.

Let's build something that lasts.
— David Selley

Marketing has changed—
Loyalty hasn't

What used to be a straightforward message delivered through a few trusted channels has now become a fast-moving, multi-generational puzzle. Boomers want one thing. Millennials want something else. Gen Z? They speak a whole different language. And Gen Alpha is coming up fast with expectations we haven't even begun to meet.

For years, we've watched businesses struggle to stay relevant—not because they weren't good at what they do, but because they didn't see the shift happening. Or worse, they saw it and didn't know how to respond.

That's where Generational Marketing—or **GenMar**, as we've come to call it—makes all the difference.

This book isn't about trendy gimmicks or one-size-fits-all campaigns. It's about something deeper: understanding the values, behaviors, and buying patterns of different generations so you can build long-term trust across age groups. It's about learning how to communicate with people where they are—not where you wish they were.

It's not easy. But it's possible. And the businesses that figure it out will dominate their markets—not just now, but for decades to come.

FOUNDATIONAL INSIGHT
What Is Generational Marketing—and What Exactly Is GenMar?

Why did one lipstick fly off the shelves while another—made with the same formula—collected dust?
It wasn't the product.
It wasn't the price.
It was the message.

You can have the best team, the best packaging, and the best product—and still fail miserably if you're speaking to the wrong generation in the wrong way.

That's not something I learned from a textbook. I learned it in real-time—through product launches, focus groups, marketing wins, and more than a few flops. Especially in the cosmetics world, success often comes down to emotion, identity, and timing—not just features and benefits.

That's the heart of **Generational Marketing.**

It's about understanding how people's life experiences shape the way they see the world—and how they make decisions. It's recognizing that what builds trust with a Baby Boomer might fall flat with Gen Z. It's not just about marketing to people, but marketing through the lens of when and how they were shaped.
Over time, I started noticing consistent patterns:

- Why packaging that felt "fresh" to a 29-year-old seemed "cheap" to someone in their 60s

- Why a message that resonated with one group left another cold

- Why strong products still failed—*not* because they were bad, but because they were communicated in the wrong generational language

That insight—being able to adjust your message, tone, visuals, and even pricing based on the generation you're serving—became a cornerstone of how I approached business. It's what I now refer to as *The GenMar Strategy.*

What Is GenMar?

As I began shaping the stories and lessons that would become this book, I realized the need for a name—a practical term that could tie together the real-world application of Generational Marketing.

That's when I coined **GenMar**—short for **Generational Marketing**. It's not a theory. It's a working strategy based on experience, results, failures, and real consumer behavior. So while Generational Marketing is the concept, GenMar is the framework—a way to make it usable, repeatable, and relevant across industries.

You'll see this term throughout the book—in sections like:

- **GenMar Strategy**
- **GenMar Takeaways**
- **GenMar Lens**
- **GenMar Adjustments**

These aren't buzzwords. They're tools to help you apply what you're learning in a way that makes sense for *your* brand and *your* audience.

And while many of the examples come from cosmetics, the *GenMar Strategy* applies far beyond. It's for *real estate, coaching, tech, education, product manufacturing, service or hospitality industries and healthcare*—anywhere you serve more than one generation of customers.

Because no matter what you sell, you're selling to people. And people are shaped by the times they've lived through.

GenMar is my name for what Generational Marketing looks like in action. Not a trend, Not a tactic. A strategy for the long haul.

Coming Soon

We're currently finalizing the **GenMar Toolkit** — a practical program to help readers apply the strategy shared in this book.

To be notified when it launches,
see the final page for details.

TABLE OF CONTENTS

TABLE OF CONTENTS (continued)

TABLE OF CONTENTS (continued)

PART ONE
The Billion-Dollar Blind Spot

Why Most Brands Fail to Capture a Lifetime Customer

A lesson born on the train to a new life. March 23, 1963

It's hard to describe the excitement and anticipation coursing through me. This wasn't just another train ride—it was the beginning of everything. I had dreamed of coming to America for as long as I could remember, and now here I was, rolling past immigration with a suitcase full of ambition and a head full of dreams. The United States wasn't just a destination. It was possibility.

What I couldn't have known then was that within a few short years, I'd be working for one of the most iconic brands in the world—Revlon. A name that seemed untouchable from the outside. Recognized everywhere. Admired by many.

But as I would learn from the inside, even the biggest brands can suffer from a billion-dollar blind spot: they focus on the moment and forget the meaning.

They chase trends but ignore the generational shifts shaping how people buy, trust, and remain loyal. Revlon, for all its fame, was built more on style and spark than on substance that could span generations. And that realization became one of my earliest lessons in the importance of Generational Marketing—what I now call the **GenMar Strategy**.

Setting the Stage
This Isn't a Marketing Trend — It's a Mindset Shift

I didn't set out to write a marketing book. I've spent most of my life building businesses, not writing about them. But over time, a pattern started to bother me—something I saw play out again and again, across industries, continents, and decades. Great companies were failing. Not because they lacked money. Not because their products weren't good. But because they didn't understand their customers—not really. They were too focused on selling something now, and not nearly focused enough on building something that would still matter ten, twenty, even fifty years later.

3

They didn't have a marketing problem. They had a philosophy problem. Worse yet, they had a **generational blind spot**—a failure to see how customers grow, evolve, and change across time.

That's why I created the **GenMar Strategy**—a practical, story-driven framework for understanding how to build lasting trust by marketing *through the lens of generations*, not just moments. GenMar isn't about chasing trends, exploiting algorithms, or jumping on the latest social media bandwagon. It's about creating **generational trust**—and earning it over time. It's about designing a brand that grows *with* your customer, not past them. It's about building a business that not only survives this generation, but connects with the next.

If that sounds like the kind of business you want to build, you're in the right place. In this book, you'll learn why some companies quietly earn loyalty generation after generation, why others collapse under the weight of short-sightedness, how to apply real-world insights from the front lines of marketing, and how to think long-term in a world obsessed with the now.

If I've done my job, you won't just walk away with new strategies—you'll walk away seeing your customer, your brand, and your legacy through a very different lens. This is where the shift begins. Let's get started.

— *David Selley*

Chapter 1

The Disconnect

Why Good Brands Fail When They Speak the Right Message to the Wrong Generation

Featuring:
Revlon vs. Estée Lauder

For years, I watched brands rise and fall from the inside out—many in the beauty industry, where image is everything… until it isn't. One thing became painfully clear: You can't build loyalty with lipstick alone. You have to understand how people evolve—how a teenager becomes a woman with different values, priorities, and buying behaviors. That shift is where most brands fall apart.

I saw it firsthand at Revlon. And I saw it done differently at Estée Lauder. Let me show you what happens when a brand talks at a generation instead of growing with them.

Case Study: **Revlon**

It looked like a success. Strong product. Slick packaging. Massive ad campaign. But a few months in, it was clear: the launch was a dud. Sales were flat. Excitement fizzled fast. The message missed.

That wasn't unusual at Revlon. I know—I was there. I came to America with a suitcase of ambition and landed inside one of the world's most glamorous brands. Revlon had a strong visual identity and fast product cycle. But in hindsight, our trend-driven launches sometimes came at the expense of deeper, long-term customer connection.

We were brilliant at grabbing attention—but not at keeping it. While we chased the next big launch, our customers quietly moved on.

This wasn't a product problem. This was a generational blind spot. We weren't listening to what customers wanted now— or who they were becoming next.

Case Study: **Estée Lauder**

While Revlon stayed loud and glossy, Estée Lauder took a different approach. Their ads weren't over-produced. Their packaging didn't scream. But their customers kept coming back—year after year, generation after generation.

They weren't just building for now. They were building for next.

Lauder understood emotional loyalty — vertical and horizontal. They adapted messaging for age groups, lifestyle shifts, and identity changes. That's what GenMar is all about.

A Little Backstage History to Set the Stage

Let me take you back to how Estée Lauder started her billion-dollar brand.

It wasn't flashy campaigns or polished displays. It was courage and vision. She launched nationally by selling twelve half-ounce bottles of Youth Dew perfume—and promised each buyer exclusive rights to future product lines.

That confident promise created trust and anticipation—long before the rest of the line existed.

Revlon's Charles Revson was livid. But Estée wasn't trying to outsell him. She was playing the long game. And that early move said everything about the brand she was building.

Estée Played the Long Game

Estée Lauder understood that a customer at 20 could become a lifelong brand advocate at 40. She built product ladders that aged with her audience. She updated tone, visuals, and storytelling with each generational shift.

She spoke to transformation—not just trends.

While Revlon focused on visual appeal and trend, Estée Lauder focused on building long-term emotional loyalty.

Flash vs. Framework

REVLON	ESTĒE LAUDER
Flash	**Framework**
• **Tactical Promotions**. Short-term campaigns focused on immediate boosts	• **Strategic Branding**. Long-term vision emphasizing brand heritage a customer loyalty
• **Product-Centric Marketing**. Highlighting individual products without cohesive brand	• **Customer-Centric Approach**. Building relationships through consistent messaging quality
• **Reactive Strategy**. Responding to market trends and competitor moves	• **Proactive Strategy**. Setting trends and leading with innovation
• **Limited Customer Engagement**. Minimal focus on building a community or	• **Strong Customer Loyalty** Fostering a loyal customer base through consistent value delivery

The $12 Billion Blind Spot

Ask anyone why Revlon has had some troubles and you'll hear the same surface answers which led to a bankruptcy and a reorganization a few years ago.

The truth? We were speaking to the wrong generation in the wrong way.

Boomers didn't buy the flash. Gen X was skeptical. Millennials tuned out. Gen Z didn't even know we existed.

While Estée evolved, Revlon faced some serious challenges. There may have been some marketing strategies that failed. Regardless of what or why things happened the result was "bankruptcy." Hopefully with its reorganization the brand will regain its previous dominance.

GenMar Insight

Brand failure isn't about the wrong product—it's about the wrong emotional message for the generation you're trying to reach.

Generational trust is earned through consistency, not just creativity. The GenMar Strategy exists to help you spot these disconnects before your customers walk away.

Wisdom Worth Repeating

"You can have the best product in the world, but if you're speaking the wrong language, no one will hear you."
— David Selley

Ask Yourself This

• Are you selling something they want today—or building trust for tomorrow?
• Have your customers grown, but your message hasn't?

• Is your brand evolving with your audience—or forcing them to outgrow you?

David's Takeaway

"A great product can start a conversation. But only a strategy behind that message keeps the conversation going—across generations."

Chapter 2

Vanity vs. Vision

The Brands That Chased the Flash —
and the Ones That Built for Legacy

❀

Featuring:
**Max Factor,
Charles of the Ritz,
Estée Lauder**

When I look back at the brands I admired—and even competed with—I realize how many of them bet everything on flash. Prestige. The "wow" factor. And for a while, it worked.

But the thing about glamor? It doesn't age well on its own. If your brand has no plan to evolve, the shimmer fades. Fast.

What They Had	What They Built (or Didn't)	
What They Had	**What They Missed**	**What They Built (or Didn't)**
Max Factor	Long-term customer relationships and luxury market presence	Struggled to adapt to changing consumer preferences
Charles of the Ritz	Consistent brand identity and family business longevity	Brand faded and company diversified unsuccessfully
Estée Lauder	Mass-market-appeal and cutting-edge innovation	Mass-market-appeal and cutting-edge innovation

I saw this up close in the fall of one of the most glamorous names in the business—Max Factor. And I watched it again in the quiet decline of Charles of the Ritz—a brand with innovation, but no forward motion.

✅

Case Study:
Max Factor

The Hollywood legend that leaned too hard on nostalgia—and paid the price.

Plenty of beauty brands rose to fame with flashy campaigns, celebrity endorsements, and stunning visuals. For a while, it worked. But what many of them failed to understand was this: vanity creates buzz—vision creates longevity.

I watched more than one brand crumble under the weight of short-term thinking. Max Factor was one of them.

It was legendary. Hollywood loved it. The Westmore brothers made it famous on the silver screen, and the Max Factor name became synonymous with glamor and celebrity. But behind the curtains, things were falling apart. Their marketing leaned on nostalgia, which proved challenging when the industry evolved rapidly.

I'll never forget the day that chapter of the company's legacy came to a close. Paul Maturzo, a dear friend of mine and President at the time, called me from Hollywood. His voice shook. He had to face the staff and announce that the company was closing its doors. He asked me to come down—to stand with him. Not as a consultant. Just as a friend.

He knew it wasn't just a company ending. It was a generation of glamor that hadn't planned for the next.

It's tempting to believe that recognition will carry your brand forever. But without relevance, recognition becomes a memory—not momentum.

✓

Case Study:
Charles of the Ritz

Ahead of their time—but left behind without a long-term vision.

Another perfect example was Charles of the Ritz—a brand that actually had one of the most innovative offerings in the industry: custom-blended face powder, made to order on the spot.

It was bold. Personalized. Experiential. They understood that beauty is emotional and unique to each person. But their vision never extended past their product counter. Their marketing never expanded beyond a single generation.

They had an incredible foundation, but no long-term map. Eventually, they were left behind—not because customers didn't want what they offered, but because no one told the story in a way that resonated with newer generations.

Compare that to what Estée Lauder was doing at the same time—and the difference becomes clear.

✓

Case Study:
Estée Lauder

The long-game brand that evolved with its customers. Estée didn't have the celebrity flash. But they had vision. They built systems that grew with their customer. They didn't just market beauty. They marketed relationship.

Their message changed as their audience changed and grew bigger. The packaging, the tone, even the ad copy evolved over time—as they went vertical and horizontal because they were watching, listening, and adjusting to generational cues, welcome the fabulous G.W.P (gift with purchase phenomenon}. That's what vision looks like.

Wisdom Worth Repeating
"Legacy is built by listening to change — not resisting it."
— David Selley

GenMar Insight
Vanity fades. Generational vision lasts.

Brands that stay relevant don't just look the part—they listen, adjust, and evolve with their customers as they age, grow, and change.

Ask Yourself This
• Are you marketing based on who your customer used to be?
• Does your brand feel modern to all generations—or stuck in the past?
• Are you leaning on nostalgia—or adjusting your message to meet the mindset of a changing customer?

David's Takeaway
"Vanity fades fast. But a clear, evolving message will carry your brand through the next decade—and beyond."

Chapter 3

Marketing from 9 to 90

How to Grow with Your Customer Instead of Losing Them by 30

✻

Featuring:
**Bonne Bell,
Jane Cosmetics,
Estée Lauder**

There's something incredibly special about being someone's first brand.

Whether it's a girl's first lipstick, a young man's first cologne, or a teen's first skincare product — it creates a connection. A memory. A moment.

But if your brand doesn't grow with that person, you become nothing more than a phase they outgrew.

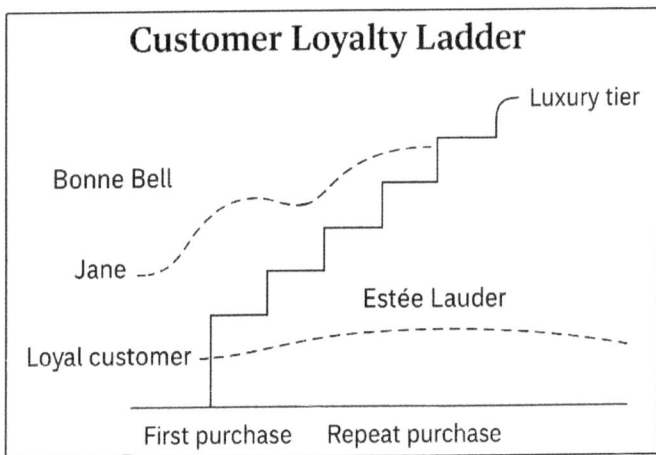

Customer Loyalty Ladder

I saw this play out again and again — not just in cosmetics, but in every consumer category. Loyalty gets built early, but sustained loyalty only happens when your brand grows up alongside your customer.

Case Study:
Bonne Bell
The youth icon that failed to grow up with its customers.

If there was ever a brand that owned the teen market, it was Bonne Bell. They had flavor. They had fun. They had Lip Smackers—those tiny, sugary tubes of scented lip balm that every middle schooler from the '70s through the '90s kept in their backpack or locker.

It was a brilliant entry point for brand loyalty. But it never led anywhere.

As those girls grew into women, their needs changed. They didn't want bubblegum-flavored gloss anymore—they wanted clean ingredients, neutral tones, elegant packaging. Bonne Bell didn't evolve. They remained connected to the entry-level phase but didn't provide a next step for customers as they matured.

You can create an unforgettable first impression, but it needs to be followed by a strategy that grows with the customer

Case Study:
Estée Lauder
*How one company created a ladder to
keep customers for life.*

Estée Lauder understood that their customers wouldn't stay

19 forever. So they created a product ladder that gave them somewhere to go. You'll see this ladder again in more detail later—but here's where it begins:

Estée Lauder didn't try to keep one product relevant for everyone. They built a system that grew with their customers:

- Clinique for the skincare-curious and entry-level buyers
- Estée Lauder for mid-market, aspirational customers
- La Mer for those who wanted the prestige, science, and status

It wasn't just a product line—it was a path forward. That's what vertical marketing does. It builds not just products—but a path.

Wisdom Worth Repeating
"People don't stop needing you—
they just stop seeing you as relevant."
— David Selley

GenMar Insight
You don't lose customers because they grow up. You lose them because you didn't grow with them.

A vertical brand doesn't just sell—it stays. It meets the customer at each life stage with messaging that feels just right, just in time.

Ask Yourself This
- Do your customers have anywhere to go next within your brand?
- Are you only selling to who they are today—or who they'll become?

• Is your product line designed to age with your audience—or are you handing them off to your competitors?

David's Takeaway

"Brands that stay relevant don't just change. They plan to. That's how loyalty becomes legacy."

Chapter 4

Loyalty Is Earned, Not Assumed

Why Customers Leave Quietly — and What Makes Them Stay

�֍

Featuring:
Jean Naté
Frances Denney

If there's one thing I've learned that still gets ignored in boardrooms, it's this:

Loyalty is never guaranteed.

I've seen too many brands assume their customers would stay simply because they always had. They thought that being "familiar" was enough. That a good product and a strong name would hold attention forever. It won't.

There are many great brand exceptions. Here are a few – Harley, Bass Pro, Kenworth Trucking, Peterbilt, Northface. Neutrogena.

Loyalty is a relationship. And like any relationship, it needs attention, renewal, and relevance. The minute you take it for granted, you begin to lose it.

Not in a dramatic exit. Not with fireworks. But quietly. Gradually. Until one day, the customer simply doesn't come back.

✅

Case Study:
Jean Naté
The scent that stayed in memory—while the brand faded away.

Jean Naté was a staple in American homes. The scent was refreshing, iconic. It was more than a product—it was a memory: summer visits, Mother's Day gifts, a post-shower ritual. People didn't just like it—they remembered it. And yet, the brand disappeared.

Not because the formula changed. Not because people stopped liking it. But because the message stopped evolving. The packaging never changed. The story was never updated. There was no emotional invitation to the next generation.

Customers didn't make a scene. They didn't organize a protest. They just... stopped buying.

I saw it up close in meetings where legacy brands believed their story was "timeless." They didn't see that what felt timeless in the '80s felt invisible in the 2000s. When the message doesn't change, loyalty doesn't vanish—it slips away while you're not looking.

Case Study:
Frances Denney

A respected name in beauty education that forgot to re-engage.

Frances Denney was once a name you couldn't ignore in professional circles. They weren't just selling makeup—they were training the next generation of estheticians. They had built a relationship that extended beyond product to purpose.

But as the world changed, they didn't. New beauty professionals started gravitating toward brands that felt modern. That looked fresh. That spoke their language.

Frances Denney held on to their reputation but didn't invest in refreshing the connection. They assumed their past would carry their future. It didn't.

They had everything they needed to win—an audience, a platform, a mission—but they stopped talking to their evolving customer. And loyalty, once again, quietly walked away.

Wisdom Worth Repeating
"You don't lose customers all at once. You lose them inch by inch—every time you assume they're still listening."
— David Selley

GenMar Insight
Loyalty doesn't die in a moment. It fades over time—when your message stops mattering to the customer you once knew so well.

GenMar teaches us to track emotional relevance, not just repeat past success.

Ask Yourself This
• Are you relying on what worked—without checking if it still connects?
• Have you given your loyal customers anything new to remember you by?
• Is your brand a memory... or still part of their everyday life?
• Have you re-earned their attention – or are you coasting on yesterday's relationship? Do you know if they really care?

David's Takeaway
"Loyalty isn't a memory—it's a moving target. Smart brands track it."

Chapter 5

Building Brands
That Outlive You

How to Create a Business That Thrives Without You in the Room

✳

Featuring:
Alexander de Markoff
Prince Matchabelli
Frances Denney

There comes a point in every entrepreneur's life where you ask yourself a tough question: What happens to the business when I'm no longer running it?

I've asked myself that many times.

When I was younger, I wanted my name attached to everything. That was ego talking. But with age and experience came clarity: a great business isn't built on one person's name—it's built on one person's vision that can be carried forward by others.

Legacy isn't about being remembered. It's about building something that still matters when you're not in the room. And some of the most "iconic" brands I worked with never figured that out.

✅

Case Study:
Alexander de Markoff
Prestige without progression—the high-end brand that stayed stuck.

Alexander de Markoff was once a symbol of exclusivity — refined, elegant, expensive. The products were beautifully packaged, the formulas high-end. It was the brand of choice for women who wanted to feel sophisticated and elite with products that promised and performed.

But prestige doesn't build loyalty if it doesn't evolve. And it doesn't attract the next generation if it doesn't make room for them.

As the market shifted and new consumer voices emerged, de Markoff didn't shift. They held tight to the high-gloss image, speaking only to the same aging clientele. There was no ladder. No modern entry point. No new emotional connection.

The result? A brand that stood still while the world moved forward.

That same blind spot shows up in brands that had every reason to endure—but still fell silent.

✓

Case Study:
Prince Matchabelli
Elegance without evolution—a royal brand that lost its reign.

Prince Matchabelli was once known for its regal aesthetic—fragrance bottles shaped like crowns, messaging steeped in old-world charm. It felt royal. It felt important. It had style. But even style has to move with the times.

Their message didn't change. The tone stayed grand and distant, even as modern consumers shifted toward authenticity, relatability, and emotional connection. Matchabelli had image—but no evolving message. Legacy wasn't built into the foundation. And when the nostalgia wore off, there was nothing left to hold attention.

✓

Case Study:
Frances Denney

A chance to build legacy from within—missed by a brand that had it all.

Frances Denney had something rare: influence. Not just over customers, but over professionals. Their name meant something in the world of estheticians, beauty schools, and salon retail.

They had built trust. They had a following. They had trained thousands of people. But they never built the next generation of that story.

Instead of creating brand ambassadors for life, they left graduates with no emotional ties or updated touchpoints. The brand stood still. It assumed people would keep referring back to it—without giving them a reason to.

I've said this before, and I'll say it again: If your brand can't survive without you, it was never really built—it was borrowed.

Wisdom Worth Repeating
If your brand can't survive without you,
it was never really built—it was borrowed."
— David Selley

GenMar Insight
A generational brand isn't tied to a personality—it's tied to a purpose.

If you want your work to outlive you, your brand must speak to more than your voice. It must speak to your values—and repeat them through time.

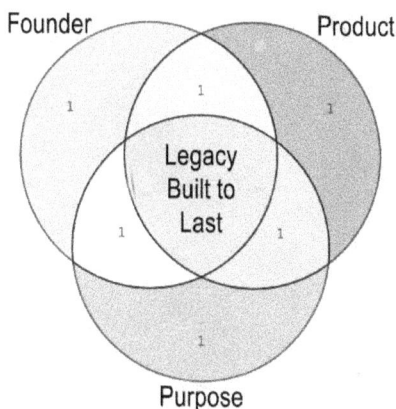

Ask Yourself This
• Would your brand still matter if your name was removed?
• Have you built a business, or a personality brand with no next chapter?
• Are they loyal to your personality—or anchored to a purpose they can carry forward?

David's Takeaway
"If your brand can't speak for itself, it was never built to last."

Chapter 6

Vertical Marketing

Why Brands That Don't Grow with Their Customers Eventually Get Left Behind
✳
Featuring:
Estée Lauder

One of the most dangerous assumptions in business: "If we get them young, they'll stick with us." They won't. Not unless you give them something to grow into.

I've seen brands invest millions into capturing the first-time buyer—especially in cosmetics. Young skin, starter makeup, beginner-friendly formulas. But they stop there. They win the first sale... and then lose every sale after.

Vertical marketing solves that problem. It's about creating a ladder that your customer can climb as their life changes. Not just new products, but new messaging. Not just pricing tiers, but emotional tiers.

Get this wrong, and you become a brand they "used to use." Get it right, and you keep customers for decades.

What Is a Brand Ladder?
A brand ladder is a strategy that grows with your customer—offering them the next level of product, message, or experience as their life evolves.

Rather than staying static or losing customers when their needs change, a ladder keeps trust intact by giving them somewhere to go within your brand. It's not just about age. It's about emotional maturity, lifestyle changes, and identity shifts. You're not selling something new. You're inviting them to stay.

Product Loyalty Ladder

LA MER

CLINIQUE

ESTEE

✓

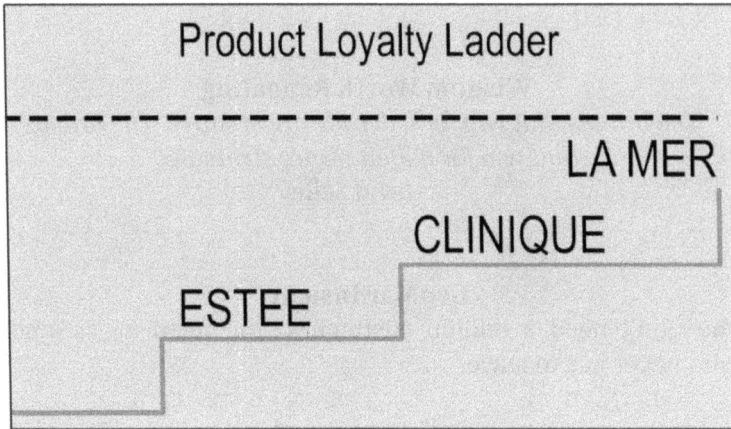

Case Study:
Estée Lauder
*The brand that built an on-ramp and a
highway for lifetime loyalty.*

Estée Lauder didn't just sell makeup. They built a system—an ecosystem, really—for keeping the customer in the brand family for life.

It started with Clinique — clean, approachable, dermatologist-tested. Perfect for teens or young adults just learning how to care for their skin. Then came the core Estée Lauder line— more elegant, aspirational, mid-market. And for those who wanted to elevate further. Prestige lines like La Mer offered luxury, science, and status.

Same customer. Three very different messages for three different life stages. That is vertical marketing. And it is one of the most underused tools in business today.

Wisdom Worth Repeating
"The brands that win for a decade are creative. The brands that win for a lifetime are strategic."
— David Selley

GenMar Insight
You don't need a million customers. You need a customer who never has to leave.

Vertical marketing is about walking alongside your customer—not just welcoming them once and hoping they stick around. If you don't show them the next step, they'll go find it somewhere else.

Ask Yourself This
• Does your brand have a "next step" for your customer—or just a welcome mat?
• Are you speaking only to who they are today, or who they're becoming?
• Is your message built to shift with their needs—or will it age out before they do?

David's Takeaway
"If your customer has to grow without you, they'll grow past you. Strategy keeps them close."

Chapter 7

Horizontal Marketing

Stretching Your Message Across Lifestyles Without Losing Your Identity

✖

Featuring:
Dana, Jane Cosmetics (revisited), and Estée Lauder

Most brands want to grow. That's not the problem. The problem is they try to grow wide... before they've grown deep.

I've seen it happen firsthand—brands that chase trends, jump into new audiences, or dilute their message in hopes of grabbing market share. But instead of expanding their reach, they erode their trust.

Horizontal marketing is about expanding your reach across generations and lifestyles—but without losing the emotional core that makes your brand matter. It's not about changing your identity. It's about translating your identity into emotional languages that make sense to each audience.

Let me show you what happens when a brand tries to stretch too far—and when one does it just right.

✓

Case Study: Dana

The once-iconic brand that disappeared trying to stretch too wide.

Dana was once a premium fragrance house—elegant, sophisticated, with a distinctly European feel. Their scents were classic. Their packaging carried weight. They knew who they were. Then came the pivot.

In an attempt to appeal to a younger audience, Dana tried to "modernize." They rolled out lower-priced lines, brighter packaging, and trendier campaigns. But instead of refreshing the brand, they fractured it.

The loyal customers felt abandoned. The new customers weren't emotionally invested. And the message-- Lost in translation.

When a brand tries to be something for everyone, it often ends up meaning nothing to anyone.

Case Study: Jane Cosmetics (Revisited)

An entry brand that couldn't cross generational or lifestyle lines.

Jane was a great first-step brand—fun, affordable, built for teens. But when they tried to expand into edgier, more fashion-forward markets, they didn't have the emotional language or credibility to make the jump.

The result? Confusion. They struggled to sustain an emotional connection across generations.

Now compare that with how Estée Lauder did it — strategically, intentionally, and without losing their soul.

✓

Case Study: Estée Lauder

A brand that crossed generations and lifestyles without compromising its identity.

Estée didn't try to be everything to everyone. Instead, they created distinct expressions of the same values across multiple lifestyle lanes:

- **Estée Lauder**: classic, refined, trustworthy — ideal for midlife and older audiences

- **Clinique**: clean, science-driven, minimalist — great for wellness-focused buyers

- **MAC**: bold, artistic, edgy — perfect for Gen Z creatives and performers

- **La Mer**: indulgent, premium, status-driven — aligned with luxury consumers

Each spoke to a different segment. But every one of them carried the **emotional consistency of the Estée Lauder DNA**: quality, trust, and relevance.

Wisdom Worth Repeating
*"If your brand starts sounding like everyone else,
it'll stop sounding like you."*
— David Selley

GenMar Insight
Stretching your message only works when the emotional core stays intact.

If you expand your audience at the cost of clarity, you're not growing—you're unraveling.

Ask Yourself This
• Is your brand message still consistent across different audiences and platforms?
• Have you changed your tone so much that your original customer wouldn't recognize you?
• Can your message adapt to new lifestyles without losing its voice?

David's Takeaway
"You can speak to more people—but only if you still sound like yourself. Clarity scales. Confusion doesn't."

Chapter 8

What Loyalty Looks Like Now

GenMar in Action
Real World Brand Translations
Emotional Loyalty, Brand Behavior
and the GenMar Advantage

Note: All brand examples used in this chapter are presented for educational and illustrative purposes only. The insights shared reflect public brand behavior and are intended to support the learning objectives of The GenMar Strategy. No endorsements or criticisms are implied, and each brand mentioned is respected for its unique journey and market presence.

What does The GenMar Strategy look like when it's applied in the real world? In this chapter, we'll look at iconic and current brands that have either embraced generational loyalty—or missed the moment. This isn't about praise or criticism. It's about learning from what's worked, where brands have adapted, and what others can do to stay relevant.

We'll explore companies across industries: legacy icons, innovative disruptors, and relational brands that continue to inspire generational trust. Each one shows us what happens when you build (or fail to build) a brand that evolves with the people it serves.

Beauty Brand Evolution

My experience at Revlon gave me a front-row seat to the power of brand recognition and the importance of evolving with your audience. As one of the most iconic beauty brands in the world, Revlon built an enduring name that spanned generations. Over time, it became clear that staying emotionally connected with emerging audiences requires continuous adaptation—a valuable lesson in how even the most established brands can grow by listening and evolving.

In contrast, Estée Lauder leaned into aspirational storytelling and emotional resonance. They spoke to values, identity, and empowerment—building emotional loyalty not just through products, but through their message.

Lancôme, another legacy brand I worked closely with, navigated these shifts more smoothly. They maintained premium positioning while evolving through modern partnerships, updated packaging, and messages tailored to generational desire.

Modern beauty disruptors have pushed this evolution even further. Fenty Beauty redefined inclusivity and emotional relevance. Launched with a strong GenMar mindset.

e.l.f. Cosmetics, meanwhile, built its success through humor, affordability, and a bold digital-first strategy—especially on platforms like TikTok. Its appeal to Gen Z shows how brands win when they understand the language, values, and emotional touchpoints of a rising generation.

These brands represent the arc of emotional loyalty in action—from legacy to reinvention. And they all connect directly to my journey inside the beauty industry, where emotional branding became personal, professional, and powerful.

Emotional Loyalty in Action:
6 Core Types

In the world of GenMar, emotional loyalty doesn't come in just one form. It can be built through values, identity, community, consistency, innovation, or ease.

As you read the brand examples below, you'll see six common loyalty types in action:

1. Identity Loyalty –
rooted in self-expression and belonging

2. Heritage Loyalty –
based on generational trust and legacy

3. Service Loyalty –
created through consistent, human-centered experiences

4. Values Loyalty –
driven by shared beliefs and mission

5. Convenience Loyalty –
built through frictionless, personalized systems

6. Co-Creation Loyalty –
developed through community involvement and shared brand voice

Each emotional loyalty type supports long-term connection across generations. Brands that master even one create customers who stay—not just buy.

Identity Loyalty
Harley-Davidson:
The Power of Identity

Harley-Davidson is a case study in emotional branding done right. They don't just sell motorcycles and noise —they sell freedom, rebellion, and belonging. Across multiple generations, Harley riders feel part of a tribe. The logo, the roar, the lifestyle—it's all emotional. This is a GenMar win: consistent messaging that connects deeply with customers from their 20s to their 70s.

Glossier:
Gen Z Loyalty Through Voice

This beauty brand speaks Gen Z's language: authentic, inclusive, casual. Their community built the brand—through comments, selfies, and reviews. They understood that emotional loyalty today comes from co-creation, not just advertising. That's GenMar applied to a new generation.

LEGO:
Multigenerational Magic

LEGO's ability to stay relevant for decades stems from their embrace of creativity, co-creation, and generational bridging. From parent-child building to collector sets, LEGO is one of the best examples of emotional loyalty through product evolution.

Heritage Loyalty
Ford Trucks:
Generational Trust on Wheels

The Ford F-Series has remained the best-selling truck in America for decades—not by accident. Their branding speaks directly to hard work, legacy, and pride. It's often generational: fathers pass down their Ford loyalty to their sons and daughters. That's emotional loyalty in motion.

John Deere:
Loyalty in Simplicity

With minimal advertising flash, John Deere has become a generational icon in farming, landscaping, and lifestyle branding. Their brand stands for reliability and value. People wear the logo with pride, not because it's trendy, but because it means something to them and their family. That's long-haul GenMar success.

Peterbilt, Kenworth & Mack Trucks:
Blue Collar Pride

These brands have become identity markers for truck drivers. The loyalty isn't about specs—it's about story. Drivers talk about their rigs like partners. These brands embody pride, purpose, reputation and top performance. Their customers become brand advocates for life.

Service Loyalty
Chick-fil-A:
Loyalty Through Service

Chick-fil-A has created deep brand loyalty by sticking to one thing: a consistently kind, service-driven customer experience. No matter your age, the experience feels dependable and positive—something many brands overlook in the digital age.

JCPenney:
A Brand at the Crossroads

Once a staple for middle America, JCPenney was trusted for price, service, and family shopping. As digital competitors rose, the brand struggled to clearly reposition itself. This isn't about failure—it's about opportunity. A GenMar approach could help redefine its voice for a new generation.

Values Loyalty
Patagonia:
Loyalty Through Values

Patagonia proves that brand loyalty can be driven by purpose. Their unwavering stance on environmental causes resonates deeply with Millennials and Gen Z, while still being respected by older generations. Their message is clear, and their values are consistent—a GenMar win rooted in mission.

Amway:
Relationship-Driven Loyalty

Amway has built a multi-generational integrity brand around relationships and personal trust with products that deliver. Distributors often enter through family connections and stay because of community. It's a perfect case of GenMar-style emotional loyalty and long-term retention.

Dove:
Campaigns That Connect Across Generations

Dove has built trust through campaigns focused on real beauty and self-esteem, connecting with multiple generations on emotional, personal levels. Their brand represents more than soap—it reflects a mission that evolves with society.

Convenience Loyalty
Amazon:
Frictionless Loyalty

Amazon didn't just win because of speed or price—it won by removing friction. From one-click ordering to personalized recommendations, Amazon mastered the art of making life easier for every generation. That's not just convenience—it's emotional loyalty built on relevance.

Netflix:
Reinvention in Action

From DVDs to streaming to global content creation, Netflix has continually evolved with consumer expecta- tions. They didn't just react—they led. By tracking generational behavior and preferences, Netflix became a GenMar powerhouse of adaptation and engagement.

Trader Joe's:
Community-Centric Simplicity

Trader Joe's has built emotional loyalty without digital ads or loyalty programs. Their secret? A warm, neighborhood-store vibe, playful voice, and a product experience that feels like a discovery. Gen Z to Boomers love the authenticity.

Spotify:
Personalization Across Generations

Spotify's recommendation engine and personalized playlists make every user feel known—whether you're 17 or 67. That seamless experience, backed by evolving culture-focused content, creates deep, data-driven emotional loyalty.

Co-Creation Loyalty
Glossier (again):
Brand Built by the Community

This brand didn't just sell products—it invited its users to co-create. From Instagram feedback to user-generated reviews, Glossier shows how today's emotional loyalty often comes from inclusion and collaboration.

LEGO (again):
Created Together, Played Forever

LEGO's fan-designed sets, brand collaborations, and intergenerational play experiences have turned customers into creators. Their GenMar genius lies in the ability to evolve with every age group.

KEY TAKEAWAY:

Each of these brands—whether legacy or modern—teaches us something about emotional loyalty. Some found ways to evolve. Some stalled in transition. But all reveal how the GenMar Strategy isn't one-size-fits-all—it's a lens. A way of seeing your customer, your message, and your future through the filter of generational trust.

The brands that master this don't just survive. They lead.

PART TWO

The GenMar Strategy
How to Build, Apply and Sustain Generational Marketing Across Your Business

Most businesses talk about "strategy" like it's a single decision—a tagline, a product launch, a slick campaign. But real strategy isn't a move. **It's a mindset.** And the *GenMar*

Strategy isn't just for marketing departments—it's for every moment your brand interacts with a customer.

It shows up in how you greet someone, how you respond to an email, how you design a package, and how you build a team that communicates with clarity, not confusion.

If Part One opened your eyes to the blind spot...PART TWO *hands you the map.*

This is where we shift from awareness to action. You'll see how GenMar thinking can be embedded into every decision you make—whether you're launching a product, training your team, or rebuilding trust with a customer base that's quietly tuning out.

We'll walk through:
- How brands evolve (or die) based on their ability to grow with their customers

- How emotional loyalty is created—not just earned once, but sustained across decades

- And how to make GenMar a living language inside your brand—not just a buzzword in your next meeting

Whether you're running a solo operation or leading a thousand-person team, this section will give you the tools, mindset, and message discipline to turn the GenMar Strategy into your most valuable competitive edge.

> *"Clear communication isn't just good practice—it's the foundation of trust and success."*
> — David Selley

Chapter 9

Buying Habits Across Generations

Why Understanding
Generational Behavior
Is the Key to Long-Term Relevance

What they buy is important.
But why they buy is everything.

One of the most common marketing mistakes is assuming all customers make decisions the same way. That a 25-year-old and a 55-year-old care about the same things, trust the same signals, and respond to the same message. They don't.

Generational Marketing isn't just about age—it's about shared experiences that shaped beliefs. From economic shifts to technology adoption to social values, each generation developed different emotional wiring around money, trust, and loyalty.

If your brand doesn't understand that, you're not just missing opportunities—you're probably sending the wrong message entirely

Strategy and Shimmer:
Knowing When to Evolve

Revlon carved out a lasting legacy with bold visuals and trend-setting products that defined beauty for generations. Their shimmer and style were iconic—but even the most recognizable brands face a challenge when audience expectations shift.

Estée Lauder took a different path, leaning into storytelling that reflected deeper emotional values. Rather than focusing solely on product, she built connection through empowerment and identity.Both stories offer valuable lessons. Great branding isn't just about what you sell—it's about how well you stay in tune with the evolving mindset of your customer.

.

Case Study:
Cosmetics Across Generations

Let's revisit one of the clearest examples of behavior-driven buying: beauty and skincare.

These products aren't just functional—they're emotional identity tools. And identity evolves with time, age, and generational values.

Revlon kept selling shimmer to a generation that had already moved on. Estée evolved. She anticipated, not reacted. That's exactly what this chart helps us understand.

Cosmetic Brand Chart: How Generations Buy and Why

Brand	Primary Generation	Emotional Appeal	Positioning
Clinique	Gen X, Millennials	Clean, simple, safe	Dermatologist-tested, intro-tier
Estée Lauder	Boomers, Gen X	Prestige, tradition, elegance	Mid-market classic luxury
La Mer	Boomers, Gen X	Status, indulgence, science	Prestige/luxury

Brand	Primary Generation	Emotional Appeal	Positioning
Revlon	Boomers	Glamour, trend, nostalgia	Mass market, high-gloss appeal
Jane	Gen X (Teens)	Youth, affordability, fun	Starter brand, approachable
Frances Denney	Silent Gen, Boomers	Refinement, subtle luxury	Quiet prestige
Coty	Boomers, Gen X	Classic, affordability	Drugstore heritage
Fenty Beauty	Millennials, Gen Z	Inclusivity, bold identity	Trend-driven, digital-first
Glossier	Gen Z	Minimalism, authenticity, vibe	Clean and direct to consumer

What This Chart Shows:

Each brand aligned with values, not just age. They didn't try to appeal to everyone. They spoke clearly—and often boldly—to one generation's mindset.

And the ones that succeeded? They built loyalty by reflecting the customer's evolving identity.

What to Do With This Insight

Ask yourself:
• Does my current message assume all customers think the same?
• Am I using the same tone and media across generations?
• Is my brand tied to a moment... or to a movement?

GenMar Action Step

Try this exercise with your own business.
Create your own version of the chart:

• What generation are you best aligned with today?
• Which one are you currently ignoring?
• What values do you need to speak to that you haven't?

The clearer you are on generational drivers, the better your message will resonate—and the longer your customers will stay with you.

This chapter is your bridge between foundational GenMar concepts and tactical strategy. It brings in real-world behavior patterns, sets up your Brand Chart, and gives you a concrete view of how different generations make buying decisions— and, more importantly, why they make them.

GenMar Insight

You don't need a different brand for every generation.
You need a different conversation for each one.

What Shapes a Generation's Buying Habits?
Every generation is influenced by:
• World events (recessions, pandemics, wars, cultural revolutions)
• Technology (digital vs. analog, instant vs. delayed gratification)
• Social values (individualism, sustainability, inclusion, authority)
• Media (TV, Instagram, TikTok, email, printed flyers)

These inputs form what I call "emotional buying defaults." Some want prestige. Some want purpose. Some want proof. You don't just sell them a product. You speak to their worldview—whether you realize it or not.

Now that we've looked at what people buy—and why—let's talk about what happens when you ignore the signals. Because sometimes, the customer tells you what they want... before they even know it themselves.

That's where we're headed next in Chapter 10.

Wisdom Worth Repeating
"If you don't know why they're buying, you'll never know why they stopped."
— David Selley

GenMar Insight
You don't need a different brand for every generation. You need a different conversation for each one.

David's Takeaway
"Generations don't just buy differently—they believe differently. Loyalty comes from showing them you understand the world they live in."

Chapter 10

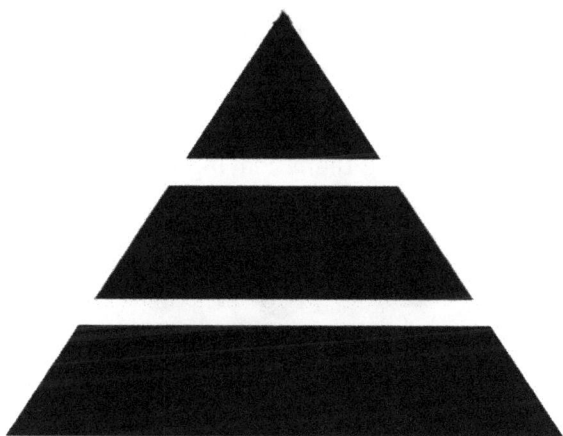

The Risk of
Playing It Safe

Why Playing Not to Lose
Is the Fastest Way to Fade Out
Featuring:
Coty, Holiday Magic
Estée Lauder

There's a moment in every brand's life when fear takes over. You've had some wins. You've built recognition. And now you're afraid to mess it up.

So you stop trying new things. You stay in the middle. You play it safe. That's how brands die.

The irony? Most brands don't fail from taking risks. They fail from avoiding them. Playing it safe doesn't protect your brand—it puts it to sleep.

Case Study:
Coty

A beauty powerhouse that got caught in neutral. Coty was everywhere. You couldn't walk through a drugstore or beauty aisle without seeing something from them—fragrance, nail polish, skincare, hair color. They were never flashy. Never high-end. But they were present.

The problem? They got too comfortable. While other brands evolved—launching new lines, refreshing packaging, or tapping into emotional trends—Coty doubled down on what had always worked. And slowly... it stopped working.

Younger customers didn't connect with the visuals. The

messaging felt dated. And the product range, while wide, lacked focus or storytelling. By staying familiar and consistent, Coty's message became harder to distinguish among a rising wave of emotionally resonant brands.

Stability is only an asset if it doesn't lead to stagnation. Otherwise, you're just treading water while others swim ahead.

✅

Case Study:
Holiday Magic

Holiday Magic was a bold experiment in cosmetics and entrepreneurship, growing rapidly through its multi-level business model in the 1960s and 70s. The company offered a compelling promise of success, beauty, and independence at a time when many were looking for a new path.

However, like many fast-scaling brands, it struggled to deepen emotional trust with customers over time. When regulation and scrutiny of the MLM industry increased, Holiday Magic faced serious challenges. Without a strong brand foundation to weather those shifts, the business was unable to sustain its early momentum.

It's a powerful reminder that surface appeal must be backed by lasting relevance and emotional connection.

✅

Case Study:
Estée Lauder

A brand that evolved through discomfort—and thrived

because of it. Estée didn't wait until their numbers dropped to reinvent. They didn't ignore new voices in the marketplace. They listened. They experimented. They took risks—small and large.

When younger buyers wanted simplicity, they launched Clinique. When artists wanted boldness, they launched MAC. When luxury buyers wanted something indulgent, they created La Mer.

Was every launch perfect? Of course not. But each one was a strategic risk built on the trust they had earned. They didn't play safe. They played smart. That's how they stayed relevant across generations.

Wisdom Worth Repeating
"If you play not to lose, you've already started losing."
— David Selley

GenMar Insight
Safety is not a strategy.

Growth requires calculated risks. Playing it safe is only safe... until it isn't.

Ask Yourself This
• What risks have you avoided that your competitors are already leaning into?
• Are you making decisions out of fear or opportunity?
• Is your "safe zone" really just a stall?

David's Takeaway
"Comfort zones are where brands retire. Relevance lives just outside of safe."

Chapter 11

Data Knows
Before You Do

How to Spot Generational Disconnects Before They Cost You Customers

Featuring:
Richard Hudnut
Estée Lauder
MAC

If there's one thing that's more dangerous than not having data—it's ignoring the data you already have.

I've sat in rooms with executives staring at flat numbers and telling themselves everything was fine. Meanwhile, churn was climbing, repeat purchases were dropping, and new generations weren't even glancing in their direction.

The brand wasn't failing. It was fading — quietly. And the data knew it first.

The data saw it coming long before the market reacted. That's what this chapter is about: how to use generational behavior signals before they become revenue losses.

Case Study:
Richard Hudnut

A heritage brand that didn't read the signals until it was too late.

Richard Hudnut was once the name in American beauty. Fragrance, skincare, powders — they had legacy, awareness, and elegance. But legacy becomes liability if you don't know when it's no longer connecting.

Their packaging stayed nostalgic. Their tone stayed formal. Their messaging didn't speak to younger generations who were starting to shop with values—like identity, inclusion, simplicity.

The data was there:

- Decreased engagement from under-30 buyers
- Lack of brand mentions on emerging platforms
- Fewer repeat purchases from newly acquired customers

But instead of adapting, they waited. And while they waited, they were erased from relevance.

Data is a flashlight. It won't make the decision for you—but it shows you where to look.

✓

Case Study:
Estée Lauder
MAC

A brand that follows the signals—and uses them to stay ahead.

When Estée saw a shift in younger customers, they didn't double down on what had always worked. They explored. They listened.

That's how MAC was born — out of data.

They saw a gap in self-expression. They tracked the rise in gender-fluid buying behavior. They noticed younger buyers leaning into bolder tones and digital-first branding.

So they responded—with a brand that still shared their DNA, but spoke a new emotional language.

MAC became more than a cosmetics line. It became a movement. A reflection of culture. And it continues to shift with its audience—because the team watches the signals.

Wisdom Worth Repeating
"Data doesn't lie. It whispers. And if you wait too long to listen, it'll start shouting—through lost revenue."
— David Selley

GenMar Insight
Data is emotional behavior translated into numbers.

If you ignore it, you're not just missing metrics—you're missing messages.

Ask Yourself This
• Are you tracking how each generation interacts with your brand—or assuming they all behave the same?
• What's your average customer age... and is it aging with your brand or away from it?
• What would your sales data say if it could talk back?

David's Takeaway
"Most brands wait for a sales drop before they change. But the signals start long before that. Smart brands learn to feel the shift before it breaks."

SPECIAL FEATURE

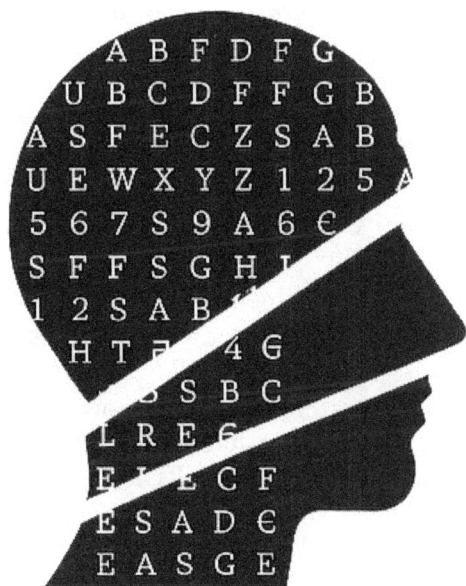

Beyond the Avatar –

Why Data Alone Can't Tell You What a Generation Believes

Let me guess—you've probably created customer avatars before.

You've named them. Dressed them. Figured out what podcast they listen to, how many kids they have, and whether they shop at Target or drive across town for organic oat milk.

I've seen some of these marketing boards. I've even built a few—back when we called them "customer types." We didn't have the fancy language back then, but we still imagined our ideal customer: she was classy, loyal, probably wore pearls on a Tuesday. And for a while? That worked.

But here's the thing:
Avatars are snapshots. GenMar is context.

You can describe a customer on paper down to her shoe size, but if you don't understand what generation she belongs to—and what shaped the way she thinks, feels, and buys—you're just guessing with better crayons.
— Avatars tell you what your customer does.
— Generational Marketing tells you what she believes.
— One's a profile. The other is a perspective.
— One shows you her shopping habits. The other shows you the cultural, emotional, and historical lens she's making those choices through.

When I worked in cosmetics, we used to build personas for our campaigns. We imagined our customer at every age—glowing skin, dependable routines, brand loyal. And for a while, our avatars matched our buyers.

Until they didn't.

Then her daughter came along—and she didn't care about "trust us, we're the experts." She wanted clean ingredients, cruelty-free testing, and brands that reflected her values. Our carefully crafted persona suddenly felt out of touch. We hadn't lost our audience... we'd ignored the next one.

That's the moment I realized something big: We weren't just losing customers. We were losing generational awareness.

This chapter isn't here to tell you avatars are wrong. They're not. They're useful tools. But if you stop there—if you build your entire brand strategy around one fictional buyer—you're missing the bigger picture.

Generational Marketing doesn't replace avatars. It reveals what avatars alone can't.

You still need the tools, the targeting, the platforms. But if you don't understand the generational values behind the behavior—what they trust, what they avoid, what emotional triggers they respond to—then your messaging is just surface-level. And surface-level doesn't last. Just like target practice, some times you hit and sometimes you miss.

GenMar Insight

When you know why a generation makes the decisions it does, you'll know how to speak to them—clearly, honestly, and in a voice they'll actually hear.

You can track behavior. But if you don't understand beliefs, you'll never build lasting trust.

Customer Avatar	GenMar Strategy
Focuses on a fictional customer	Focuses on generational traits and patterns
Tells you what they do	Reveals *why* they do it
Based on demographics and preferences	Based on values, experiences, and identity
Useful for targeting	Essential for *connecting*

Chapter 12

Seeing the
Invisible
Generations

How Overlooked Audiences Hold the Key to Lasting Loyalty.

Featuring:
**Shiseido (global Japanese beauty brand)
and Estée Lauder**

The biggest mistake brands make isn't always what they say. It's who they forget to say it to.

When I work with entrepreneurs or executives, they often tell me they "know their audience." But what they really mean is, "we know the audience we've always talked to." That's not enough.

Generational Marketing isn't just about talking to Boomers, Gen X, Millennials, and Gen Z like they're checkboxes. It's about recognizing the emotional and lifestyle patterns of groups that have been quietly ignored—or spoken to with the wrong tone.

And the moment you make a generation feel invisible, you've already lost them.

✓

Case Study:
Shiseido

A legacy brand that nearly lost the next generation—then turned it around.

Shiseido is one of the most respected names in global beauty. For decades, they led with elegance, skincare science, and prestige packaging. Their message resonated deeply with Gen

X and older Millennial buyers. But then came Gen Z.

These younger consumers weren't just looking for "nice skin." They were drawn to brands that reflected their values—like inclusivity, authenticity, and vibrant energy. While Shiseido's traditional messaging had long resonated with elegance and heritage, it didn't fully connect with this emerging generation.

Rather than resisting change, Shiseido responded thoughtfully. They introduced WASO—a skincare line designed specifically with Gen Z in mind, featuring clean ingredients, a sustainability focus, and a fresh, approachable tone. It was a smart evolution—welcoming a new audience without losing the brand's core identity.

Invisible generations aren't always young. Sometimes they're caregivers. Sometimes they're over 60. Sometimes they're men who quietly buy skincare but never see themselves in your marketing.

The question isn't, "Who are we reaching?" The question is, "Who's not here?"

Case Study:
Estée Lauder

A masterclass in seeing the full customer life cycle.

One reason Estée Lauder continues to thrive is that they don't just market to demographics. They build brand bridges that invite people across generations.

They didn't assume a woman who loved Clinique at 20 would suddenly vanish at 40. They didn't ignore the older customer who still wants to feel beautiful and relevant.

They continued to speak to them—just with new emotional cues, updated tones, and product evolutions that respected who they'd become.

When other brands forgot, Estée remembered. And that's why their customers remember them.

Wisdom Worth Remembering
"The most expensive mistake a brand can make is forgetting someone who once loved them."
— David Selley

GenMar Insight
Marketing isn't just about who you reach. It's about who you remember. And who remembers you.

Ask Yourself This
• Are there generations or customer groups that your messaging currently ignores?
• Do you have legacy customers who no longer feel spoken to?
• Is your brand actively inclusive—or just quietly repetitive?

David's Takeaway
"The customer you forget to speak to is the one you lose without even realizing it. Sometimes the biggest win is simply seeing them again with a fresh view."

Chapter 13

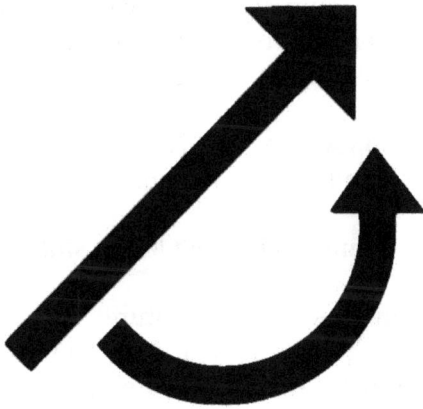

From Trends to Timeless

How to Build a Brand That Doesn't Expire with the Algorithm

Some brands chase the moment. Others create movements.

There's nothing wrong with following trends—unless that's all you're doing. In a world where marketing often lives and dies by what's "trending," the brands that last are the ones that know how to pivot without losing their point of view.

They don't just follow the wave. They know when to catch it —and when to stand still and let it pass.

Timeless Doesn't Mean Stale

A timeless brand doesn't ignore culture. It evolves with it. But it does so through intentional adaptation, not desperate reinvention. Trendy brands win attention. Timeless brands win trust.

When a message is built on something real—emotional connection, shared values, generational understanding—it holds up even when the platform, format, or algorithm changes.

You don't have to be flashy to be remembered. You have to be true, and you have to be consistent.

GenMar Insight

Trends tell you where attention is right now. Generational values tell you where trust will be tomorrow.

If you can align your brand with both, you're not just visible—you're valuable.

A Real-World Reminder

Estée Lauder didn't become a generational giant by jumping on every new idea. They did it by understanding their customers' lives. Their values. Their evolving sense of identity. They used fresh language, new product lines, and cultural awareness—but the emotional thread never broke.

Other brands copied styles. Estée built a system. And that is the difference.

By now, you've seen how Estée Lauder's strategy shows up again and again—and that's the point. It wasn't a one-time decision. It was a generational system. And it's the reason they're still here.

Don't Ditch the Trend—Just Anchor It

This chapter isn't telling you to ignore what's new. It's reminding you to build a foundation beneath it. Because if you base your brand on trends alone, you'll always be reacting. But if you build it on timeless emotional relevance, you'll always be trusted—no matter what's trending.

Chapter 14

From the Trenches –
David Selley's
Generational Lessons

Real Stories,
Real Blind Spots,
Real Growth

What Real-Life Ventures Taught Me About the Cost of Getting It Wrong (and the Power of Getting It Right)

You've seen the strategy.
Now it's time for the stories.

Before We Begin…
These stories aren't just examples—they're chapters from my life.

What you're about to read comes directly from *Papa the Entrepreneur*, a book I wrote about the ventures that shaped me—good, bad, and humbling.

I've built businesses in England, Canada, and the United States. Some made money. Others made messes. But every single one made me smarter.

Looking back now, I can see where I succeeded because I understood my audience—and where I failed because I was stuck in my own generational mindset.

These aren't "cleaned up" stories. They're real. Raw. And if I'm being honest, a little painful at times. But I share them because the lessons are still true—and if they help you avoid the same blind spots I had, then they were worth learning the hard way.

The Gourmet Chalet

*The Risk of Making Emotional Decisions
for the Wrong Audience*

I once bought a gourmet food shop in Lake Tahoe—*The Gourmet Chalet*. It sounded charming, didn't it? What I didn't realize is that charm doesn't pay the rent.

The shop was beautiful, but I'd bought it with my heart, not my head. I thought people wanted old-world elegance and specialty foods. I assumed they wanted what I would want.

But the market had changed. The visitors were younger, busier, and didn't care about British tea tins and premium preserves. They wanted convenience, not tradition. And I never stopped to ask: *"Who are we really serving now?"*

GenMar Takeaway:

I was speaking to my generation's values—not theirs.
I didn't just miss the message—
I missed the entire mindset.

84

Start Me Up Auto Product
Innovation Isn't Enough If You Don't Know the Audience

This was a device that could instantly jump- start your car battery. Smart idea. Great engineering. But I was solving a problem that my generation worried about... not the one currently driving the market.

Boomers might have cared. Gen X had AAA. Millennials and

Gen Z? Half of them didn't even *own* cars. I never thought to ask: *"Who still has this problem?"*

The product flopped—not because it didn't work, but because the *need* had already passed me by.

Technology at the auto pro-duction industry level kicked – welcome **key fob**.

GenMar Takeaway:

Even the best idea will fail if it doesn't match the emotional reality of the generation you're marketing to.

Lost & Found
The Idea That Was Ahead of Its Time

In 1964, I launched a national *Lost & Found* service—long before digital tracking. The idea was simple: mark items with a serial number so they could be returned if lost or stolen.

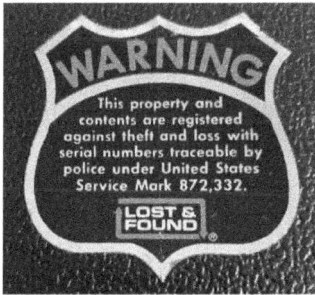

I tested it with pet ID tags, knowing how emotionally attached people are to their pets. I designed a logo, created registration cards, and left materials at local pet stores. It worked—registrations came in.

The Opportunity—and the Oversight —While selling typewriters in L.A., I met a CPA who offered connections and legal help in exchange for a share. He helped me register the trademark and set up a Bermuda-based trust.

What I didn't do? Read the fine print. I unknowingly signed away 97% of my interest. That was my first painful lesson in legal literacy.

Big Potential, No Payoff — We had meetings with Samsonite and several banks. They loved the concept—but regulations and lack of industry cooperation killed the momentum. The idea was great. But the timing—and my blind trust—were off.

GenMar Takeaway
Innovative ideas aren't enough. You need timing, legal insight, and alignment with the generation you serve. I aimed ahead—but didn't grasp the systems of the time.

Sonja's Food & Gifts
A Beautiful Store Doesn't Guarantee Loyalty

This was a high-end gift shop and English tea store I built with my wife. People loved walkng in. They complimented the design. They smiled and sipped the free samples. But compliments don't pay the bills.

The younger crowd wanted experiences. The older crowd was tightening their wallets. We had no digital presence, no scalable loyalty strategy, and no message that spoke directly to either generation. We built something lovely—but we never adapted it to who was walking through the door.

GenMar Takeaway:

If your brand identity stays the same but your audience evolves, you risk becoming forgettable—even if your product is wonderful.

Nothing Down Real Estate
When the Message Meets the Mindset, Magic Happens

This one was a win. I taught people how to buy real estate with no money down.
Why did it work?

Because I was speaking to **Gen X** — a generation skeptical of traditional wealth systems, hungry for independence, and open to creative strategies. I gave them control, showed them how to sidestep institutions, and trusted them to make it work. They ate it up. I made over $750,000 in two years.

GenMar Takeaway:
When your product and your message **match the emotional values of a generation**, you don't have to chase customers. They come to you ready.

What I Know Now
Looking back, I can see it clearly:

- When I understood the *values* of the generation I was serving, I won.

- When I marketed from *my own perspective* instead of theirs, I lost.

If I had known then what I know now, I would've made different decisions in nearly every venture. But the blessing of hindsight is that it turns into foresight—if you pay attention. *GenMar isn't a theory to me. It's a translation tool. A compass. And in many cases... a second chance.*

Want More Stories—and Strategies— from My Entrepreneurial Journey?

This chapter is just a glimpse into a larger journey—a journey that spans over eight decades, three countries, and more business ventures than most people would dare to try.

The Entrepreneur – Papa's Secrets #4
isn't just another book of stories.

It's a masterclass in entrepreneurship, told in real time, with no filters. It's written for entrepreneurs of all kinds—first-time founders, seasoned business owners, creators, inventors, and even dreamers still on the edge of starting.

Inside, you won't find theories. You'll find what actually happened—the lessons, the risks, the pivots, the partnerships, the branding decisions, and the brutal moments when things fell apart (and how I rebuilt).

This book is:
- A tool for reflection

- A roadmap of entrepreneurial decision-making

- And a self-help guide for anyone trying to build something that lasts

Whether you're running your first side hustle or your fifth company, these stories will give you a mirror and a map—so you don't have to learn everything the hard way like I did.

You can explore *The Entrepreneur – Papa's Secrets #4* and the full Papa Series at:

www.777iea.com

Real life. Real lessons. And I'm still learning.

PART THREE
Building GenWealth
Turning the GenMar Strategy into Long-Term Legacy and Leadership

Legacy Begins Now

In Part Two, we focused on reaching your audience. In Part Three, we focus on building a legacy that lasts beyond you.

Introduction

You've seen the blind spots. You've learned the strategy. Now it's time to think bigger.

Generational Marketing isn't just about clever campaigns or catching attention. It's about trust. It's about longevity. It's about building something that matters—not just today, but decades from now.

In this part of the book, we move from strategy to stewardship. From short-term engagement to long-term equity. This is where GenMar becomes GenWealth.

Not wealth in the narrow sense. But the kind that comes from emotional relevance, consistent values, and staying power.
In these final chapters, I'll show you how to apply this thinking across your leadership, your brand system, and your customer experience.

We'll cover:
• How to implement GenMar as a top-down leadership framework
• How to rebuild or refresh your brand system in 30 days
• How to train your team to speak emotional language across departments
• How to create a brand your customers pass down—not just buy from

Because your success isn't just about how many people buy from you today—it's about how many remember you tomorrow.
This isn't just about legacy as a concept. It's about building a living system that can thrive without you someday—and still feel like you.

A Quick-Check for Leaders
Before You Build for Legacy

You've learned the GenMar Strategy. You've seen what happens when brands fail to evolve. Now ask yourselfl...

Before you start building for the next 50 years—have you truly looked at your message through your customer's eyes... right now?

These rapid-fire questions are designed to spark instant awareness—tailored to your industry.

Retail & Product-Based Businesses

• Are your first-time buyers being invited into a longer relationship—or just a single transaction?

• Does your packaging and message still match the emotional reality of your customers today?

Coaches, Educators, & Thought Leaders

• Are you teaching from your own perspective —or translating for theirs?

• Is your core message aging with your audience —or leaving them behind?

Healthcare, Wellness & Service Providers

- Does your tone offer peace, empathy, and emotional safety?

- Are you speaking to what they *fear* —or what they *hope* for?

Corporate Leaders & Professional Services

- Is your tone inclusive across generations —or built for boardrooms only?

- Do your policies reflect evolving values —or legacy assumptions?

Tech, Startups & Digital Brands

- Are you building with clarity—or just cleverness?

- Are older generations opting out—not because of the product, but because of the tone?

Wisdom Worth Repeating
"The costliest mistake in business?
Thinking your audience still sees you the way they used to."
— David Selley

Chapter 15:

Building GenWealth: Where Strategy Becomes Legacy

Marketing from the Top Down
How Leaders Build Brands That Think Generationally

�֎

Featuring:
**Internal Culture, Executive Vision
GenMar in Leadership Teams**

By the time a customer sees your marketing... Your real brand has already spoken.

It shows up in how your receptionist answers the phone. How your store manager talks to a frustrated customer. How your leadership team prioritizes product features. That's why GenMar isn't just a marketing strategy. It's a leadership agency.

The best marketing doesn't start in the marketing department. It starts at the top.

For years, I watched executive teams focus all their energy on what the market was doing—while ignoring how their own internal teams were communicating (or not communicating) across generations.

They had all the right tools externally. But internally, there was no plan.And when your internal brand is out of sync, your external message falls apart—quietly and quickly.

◆

A GenMar Case
You Never See in Ads

At one company I advised, the leadership team was building a campaign targeting Gen Z—vibrant, emotional, and hyper-personalized. But when I walked into the training room, the onboarding manual felt like it was written in the 1980s. Their frontline team hadn't been briefed on the new language or brand tone. Their customer service emails still sounded robotic and corporate.

So what did Gen Z feel when they interacted with the brand? Confusion. Inconsistency. Disconnection.

That campaign didn't fail because of weak creative. It failed because the top-down vision didn't trickle down.

◆

The GenMar Strategy Isn't Optional Culture
It's Required Leadership
Generational thinking has to live in leadership conversations. Because brand consistency doesn't start with slogans—it starts with shared emotional intelligence.

If your executive team isn't asking:
• "What does this message sound like to a Millennial mom?"
• "Will this tone alienate Boomers?"
• "Are we giving Gen Z a reason to believe?"

Then you're not building a GenMar brand. You're just marketing to one.

◆

Building a Culture That Sees Generations
Here's what GenMar-aligned companies do at the leadership level:

- They train managers to understand emotional language and generational triggers
- They build onboarding systems that reinforce tone, message, and mission
- They make customer retention a top-level metric, not just a marketing KPI
- And they reward teams for creating loyalty across life stages, not just closing sales

---

Wisdom Worth Remembering
"The best campaigns are built by leaders who know how to listen across generations."
— David Selley

GenMar Insight
Generational strategy isn't a campaign you run—it's a culture you lead.
When leadership embraces it, the brand doesn't just market well—it behaves well.

Ask Yourself This
- Does your leadership team speak the same emotional language as your brand?
- Have you trained your team to live the message—or just sell it?
- Are decisions being made based on generational data—or gut instinct?

David's Takeaway
"If your brand message starts with marketing, it's already too late. Culture creates clarity—and clarity builds loyalty."

Chapter 16

The 50-Year Customer Map

How to Lead with Loyalty
Instead of Chasing the Next Sale
�֍

Featuring:
**Brand Longevity, Emotional Timelines,
GenWealth in Action**

Most brands are still chasing next quarter. The best brands? They're designing for the *next*—and the one after that.

This chapter isn't about restating what we covered before. It's about *what happens when you apply GenMar consistently across time.* Not in a campaign. Not for a product. But as a *leadership lens.*

Your customer is going somewhere. Emotionally. Financially. Mentally. The questions is will your brand still be *relevant when they get there?*

This is where GenMar becomes *GenWealth. We touched on this idea back in Chapter 5—about building a brand that can outlive you. But this isn't just about surviving without you. It's about evolving with your customer for decades to come.* Not wealth as in revenue (though that follows). Wealth as in *relevance, trust,* and *multi-decade connection.* That's what the *50-Year Customer Map* is for.

◇

What Is the 50-Year Customer Map?
It's a way to visualize the *emotional and generational journey* your customer is on—and how your brand must evolve to stay invited in.

You're no longer marketing to someone at a point in time. You're *building a relationship across time.*

This map includes:

- Life stages (teen, young adult, parent, professional, empty nester, elder)

- Emotional priorities at each stage

- How your brand's tone, product focus, and messaging must shift to meet them

Brands like Estée Lauder didn't just sell to customers. They *aged with them.* And that's why they've outlasted trends, platforms, and competitors.

◆

How GenMar Evolves into GenWealth

GenMar teaches you how to reach people. GenWealth teaches you how to *stay with them.*

A brand that understands the shifting emotional needs of each generation doesn't have to constantly reacquire customers. It gets invited back—again and again.

That's what builds *loyalty equity.*
That's what gets passed from parent to child.
That's what becomes part of someone's identity.
And that's when your brand becomes
more than a business.
It becomes a legacy.

*"A brand that evolves with you becomes
part of who you are."*
— David Selley

GenMar Insight

Long-term loyalty isn't a reward for great marketing. It's the result of staying emotionally relevant as your customer evolves.

Ask Yourself This

• Where does your customer first meet your brand—and where do you lose them?
• Do you know what matters to them today... and what they'll care about 20 years from now?
• Is your message built to evolve—or built to expire?

David's Takeaway

"Most companies map a sales funnel. Few ever map a customer's life. That is the difference between growth and GenWealth."

Chapter 17

Brand as Legacy

From Entrepreneur to Architect — How to Build Something That Outlives You
Featuring:
Succession, Emotional Equity, GenMar as a Leadership Standard

There comes a point in your journey where you stop asking: "What do I want to sell?" And start asking: "What do I want to leave behind?"

That's what this chapter is about. You've built a business. Maybe multiple. You've learned to message better, lead smarter, and reach customers in ways that resonate across generations.

But the final leap? That's where you stop building for attention—and start building for meaning.

◆

Legacy Isn't About Being Remembered
It's about being repeatable.

If your brand disappears when you retire, you didn't build a legacy. You built a job. A successful one, maybe—but not a sustainable one.

Legacy brands create systems that live beyond the founder:

• Messaging that holds together without micromanagement
• Customers who stay because of values—not personality
• A team that can speak your emotional language even when you're not in the room

That's what GenWealth really is: Value that survives your absence.

◇

The Role of the Generational Architect

You are no longer just a marketer. You are the architect of a brand experience that travels across decades.

That means thinking in structures, not just stories:

• Can your onboarding teach GenMar to new hires in 10 minutes?
• Can a 25-year-old and a 55-year-old customer both feel seen by your brand?
• Can a second-generation customer say, "My mom trusted this brand. Now I do too"?

That's the voice of brand legacy.
And it's your job to design it.

◇

From Solo Vision to Generational Culture
Legacy doesn't happen by accident. It happens when your values are turned into systems, and your strategy becomes a culture.

Ask yourself:
• Does your team know how to speak to each generation emotionally?
• Is your leadership modeling GenMar in hiring, training, and service?
• Are you building a business that someone wants to inherit?

GenMar Insight
You don't pass on a brand. You pass on a belief system—one that lives in every message, moment, and memory.

Ask Yourself This
• If you stepped away tomorrow, would your brand still sound like you?
• Have you built processes—or just preferences?
• Can your customer describe what your brand stands for without seeing your face?

David's Takeaway
"You can't force legacy. But you can design for it.
Every generational brand is built by someone who thought further than today."

Chapter 18

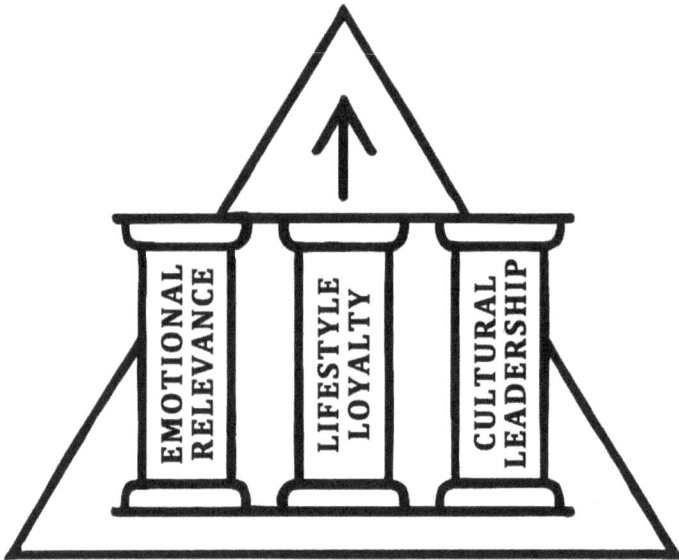

EMOTIONAL RELEVANCE

LIFESTYLE LOYALTY

CULTURAL LEADERSHIP

Your GenWealth Strategy

How to Move Forward with Clarity, Confidence, and Generational Impact

✼

Featuring:
GenMar in Action, Final Brand Audit,
Building What Lasts

You've seen the blind spot. You've learned the strategy. You've built the map. Now it's time to take the lead.

This final chapter isn't about looking back. It's about making decisions forward—as a brand, as a leader, and as someone who now sees the business through a generational lens.

GenWealth is not a theory. It's not fluff. It's what happens when GenMar becomes not just something you "apply"—but something you lead with.

This chapter gives you a way to do that—clearly, confidently, and with consistency.

Your GenWealth Strategy
Is Built on 3 Commitments:
1.
Commit to Emotional Relevance

You won't chase clicks or gimmicks. You'll build messages that match the mindsets of each generation you serve.

2.
Commit to Lifecycle Loyalty
You'll stop trying to "win the sale" and instead map the full journey. You'll design brand experiences that grow with people, not just push products.

3.
Commit to Cultural Leadership
You'll infuse GenMar into your hiring, your training, your service, and your systems. You'll make emotional clarity part of your brand culture — not just your marketing copy.

That's what turns a brand into a legacy.
That's what earns GenWealth.

Your Legacy Starts with One Decision
Most people close a business book with good ideas and a few notes. I want you to close this one with a decision:

Where does your brand need to grow emotionally right now?
Not logistically.
Not financially.
Emotionally.

That's where the real gaps hide. And that's where the GenMar Strategy gives you your edge.

Wisdom Worth Repeating
"The goal isn't just growth.
The goal is growth that lasts—and a brand that means
something when you're no longer the one saying it."
— David Selley

"If you want a customer for life, you have to stop selling to the
moment and start building for the journey."
— David Selley

GenMar Insight
GenWealth isn't a brand asset on a spreadsheet. It's a trust you've earned, the loyalty you've nurtured, and the meaning you've delivered—across decades.

Ask Yourself This
• What part of your brand needs to evolve emotionally right now?
• Who are you currently forgetting to speak to—and how can you re-engage them?
• What would your business look like if GenMar wasn't just your strategy... but your culture?

David's Takeaway
"Don't wait for a crisis to think long-term. Build for the next generation while you're still here—and let your brand live on in the hearts of those who trust it."

Chapter 19

Putting GenMar
To Work

Putting GenMar to Work

How to Apply the Strategy You've Just Learned — Even on Your Own

You've just explored a powerful set of ideas about how different generations think, buy, and trust brands. You've seen how loyalty is built — or lost — when businesses miss the mark on messaging. The good news? You can start applying what you've learned right away.

This chapter is your jumpstart. Use it as your own roadmap — and know that more advanced resources are available when you're ready to go deeper.

1

Know Who You're Talking To
Start by identifying the generations your business serves.

Think about your typical customers. Are they in their 20s? Retirees? A mix?

Try this:
- Review your sales records, email list, or social media followers.
- Pay attention to buying patterns, feedback, and even profile pictures.

- Don't guess — start observing the generational clues already around you.

2

Look at Your Brand Through a Generational Lens
How does your brand sound, look, and feel to different age groups?

Try this:
- Re-read your About page, scroll through your recent social media posts, or skim your latest email.
- Ask yourself: Would this feel *relatable* to a 28-year-old? *Trustworthy* to a 68-year-old?

Even small changes in tone or visuals can make a big difference. Think of it like adjusting your volume and lighting — same message, just presented in a way each group can actually hear and see.

3

Tweak — Don't Overhaul
You don't need a new product. You might just need a more generationally-aware presentation.

Try this:
Choose one piece of content (an ad, post, video, or page) and make a small generational shift:
- **Boomers**: Add trust signals ("In business 20+

years," "Family-owned") with clear, no-fluff language.
- **Gen X**: Be practical and direct. Explain benefits without hype.
- **Millennials**: Highlight values, purpose, and transparency.
- **Gen Z**: Keep it short, authentic, and visually engaging.

4

Take Action Today — Not Next Month

**Don't wait for a big marketing overhaul.
Start small, but start now.**

Try one of these:
- Rewrite your About page using what you've learned
- Plan a social media post designed to reach a new generation
- Film a quick "Who We Are" video that builds trust
- Rework your tagline to align with generational values

Even one meaningful update can make a noticeable impact.

5

Ready for More?

If you'd like help applying the GenMar Strategy more efficiently, we've built a suite of simple, smart tools you'll soon be able to access. From generation checkers to messaging guides, they're designed to take the guesswork out of generational marketing — and they're coming soon at **GenMarStrategyTools.com**.

You'll be able to:
- Identify your audience by generation
- Fine-tune your brand voice
- Generate copy that resonates across age groups
- Use templates, checklists, and short training prompts — no team required

Stay tuned — or visit the site to get on the waitlist.

Wisdom with a Wink and a Grin

*(A Few Things I've Learned...
and a Couple I'm Still Working On)*

These quotes didn't come from a collection—I wrote them. Most come from lessons learned the hard way (and sometimes more than once).

Some are reminders I still need myself. Others are things I say because they've stood the test of time—and a few questionable decisions.

If one of them helps you think, laugh, or sidestep a mistake, then I've done my job.

In David's Words:
Legacy Quote Vault

*Curated Wisdom from David Selley –
Shared Across Generations*

◇

*The GenMar
& GenWealth Mindset*

"You can have the best product in the world, but if you're speaking the wrong language, no one will hear you."

"Loyalty is not a line—it's a loop. And brands that close the loop across decades unlock GenWealth."

"Most brands wait for a sales drop before they change. Smart brands feel the shift before it breaks."

"You don't pass on a brand. You pass on a belief system—one that lives in every message, moment, and memory."
"You can't force legacy. But you can design for it."

"Your story is your legacy—let it inspire the world."
"Relevance is earned by those who evolve. The brand that stays emotionally aware stays invited."

"This strategy isn't for marketing departments—it's for every moment your brand interacts with a human being."

"Legacy isn't about holding on. It's about letting go—intentionally, and with clarity."

"The longer you walk with them, the fewer ads
you'll ever need."

"The costliest mistake in business? Thinking your audience
still sees you the way they used to."

"If your brand message feels 'off'—it's not always the
product. Sometimes, it's the tone."

"Am I helping them build something that lasts—or just
offering a fix for today?"

"Sometimes the smartest strategy isn't adding something
new. It's hearing something you've been missing."

◇

Entrepreneurship, Leadership,
& Impact

"Clear communication isn't just good practice—it's the
foundation of trust and success."

"Emotion may spark an idea, but only research and planning
can build a lasting business."

"The first step to entrepreneurship is knowing yourself. The
second is daring to try."

"An idea is only as strong as the effort you put into making it
safe, reliable, and valuable."

"Success isn't about standing on one pillar—it's about
building a foundation strong enough to hold your dreams."
"Passion fuels the dream, but practicality keeps it alive."

"Success isn't measured only by the ventures we build, but also by the wisdom we share and the people we empower to build their own."

"The cost of delay isn't just time lost—it's progress, potential, and peace of mind."

"Trust is the currency of every successful deal. Without it, no negotiation will stand the test of time."

"Procrastination is the mother of failure."
"Never take advice from someone who has not done what they are talking about."

$$\diamondsuit$$

On Vision, Innovation & Influencer

"It's not about breaking the rules for the sake of it; it's about seeing the world differently and daring to act on what you see."

"People with polarized opinions will only educate themselves to their level of ignorance."

"Noble effort begets noble rewards."

"A true mentor doesn't just show the way— they inspire you to carve your own path."

"Entrepreneurship knows no borders—it thrives on the power of global connections and shared ambitions."

"Adventure doesn't stop with age—it begins again with every opportunity to learn, connect, and grow."

A tribute to legacy thinking in all its forms.

◇ ◇

Legacy Words from Great Minds
Inspiration from Visionaries, Builders, and Bold Thinkers Who Shaped the World

Sometimes, someone else says it so perfectly...
you just have to pass it on.

These quotes—from business icons, inventors, mentors, and mavericks—have stood the test of time. They challenge us to think bigger, lead better, and keep going.

○ Andrew Carnegie
"The first man gets the oyster, the second man gets the shell."

○ Benjamin Franklin
"Tell me and I forget, teach me and I may remember, involve me and I learn."

○ Donald Trump
"In the end, you're measured not by how much you undertake, but by what you finally accomplish."

"Sometimes your best investments are the ones you don't make."

120

"Sometimes by losing a battle, you find a new way to win the war."

"I like thinking big. If you're going to be thinking anything, you might as well think big."

"What separates the winners from the losers is how a person reacts to each new twist of fate."

💬 Elon Musk
"Some people don't like change, but you need to embrace change if the alternative is disaster."

"When something is important enough, you do it even if the odds are not in your favor."

"I think it is possible for ordinary people to choose to be extraordinary."

"I could either watch it happen or be a part of it."

"Constantly think about how you could be doing things better and keep questioning yourself."

💬 Howard Schultz
"In times of adversity and change, we really discover who we are and what we're made of."

💬 Jeff Bezos
"If you double the number of experiments you do per year, you're going to double your inventiveness."

💬 Larry Page
"Always deliver more than expected."

💬 Mary Kay Ash
"We must have a theme, a goal, a purpose in our lives.
If you don't know where you're aiming, you
don't have a goal."

💬 Peter Thiel
"Brilliant thinking is rare, but courage is in
even shorter supply than genius."

💬 Reid Hoffman
"An entrepreneur is someone who jumps off a cliff
and builds a plane on the way down."

💬 Richard Branson
"You don't learn to walk by following rules.
You learn by doing, and by falling over."

💬 Steve Jobs
"Innovation distinguishes between a
leader and a follower."

💬 John F. Kennedy
"Ask not what your country can do for you...
but what you can do for your country."

💬 Zig Ziglar
"You can IF you think you can."

💬 Norman Vincent Peale
"Change your thoughts and you change your world."

○ Albert Einstein
"Try not to become a man of success.
Rather become a man of value."

○ Napoleon Hill
"Whatever the mind can conceive and believe,
it can achieve."

○ Peter F. Drucker
"The best way to predict the future is to create it."

These quotes make great conversation starters, social media
captions, team meeting prompts, or just quiet reminders for
when the road gets long.

Images & Illustrations
Some illustrative visuals in this book were created using
generative AI tools for conceptual clarity. They are used strictly
for educational and illustrative purposes.

"David Selley's PAPA Book Series: A Guinness World Record Journey" The PAPA Book Series

(Part of a Guinness World Record Attempt: "The Oldest Author to Publish the Most Books in One Year")

David Selley's *PAPA Book Series* is an extraordinary collection of life stories, lessons, and wisdom, part of his bold attempt to set a Guinness World Record as the **oldest author to publish the most books in a single year**. The series spans David's journey across **three continents**—as a son, father, entrepreneur, and husband—offering readers a rich tapestry of memoir and practical advice, rooted in personal experience.

At the heart of this series is not only David's vast entrepreneurial experience but also the story of his 65-year marriage, a remarkable testament to the power of love, perseverance, and partnership. Throughout the books, David reflects on how his marriage shaped his personal and professional life, offering readers invaluable lessons on building and sustaining long-lasting relation- ships, as seen in *PAPA #6: The Four Seasons of Marriage* and *PAPA #7: How to Stay Married 65+ Years*. His insights will resonate with anyone looking to navigate the evolving phases of life with grace and commitment.

Additionally, as David transitions into his latest entrepre-neurial project, the series introduces readers to the potential benefits of his International Entrepreneur Association (IEA), which aims to foster a global import/ export network. This network will create exciting new opportunities for businesses worldwide, facilitated by Executive Directors in each of the top 20 countries. By leveraging his extensive knowledge and global connect-ions, David envisions a closed system where importers and exporters can trade efficiently, creating a new revenue stream for IEA members. This groundbreaking initiative highlights how modern entrepreneurship can cross borders, providing financial growth and networking opportunities for businesses and entrepreneurs alike.

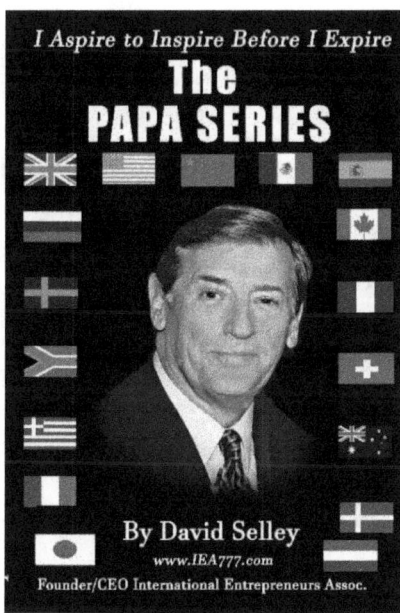

I Aspire to Inspire Before I Expire

The
PAPA SERIES

By David Selley
www.IEA777.com
Founder/CEO International Entrepreneurs Assoc.

The Papa Book Series
Celebrating the Life, Legacy, and Lessons of David Selley

Spanning three continents and a lifetime of bold choices, The Papa Book Series captures the extraordinary journey of David Selley. Each volume is a powerful standalone story of resilience, entrepreneurship, and heartfelt moments—woven together to form a legacy that inspires generations to come.

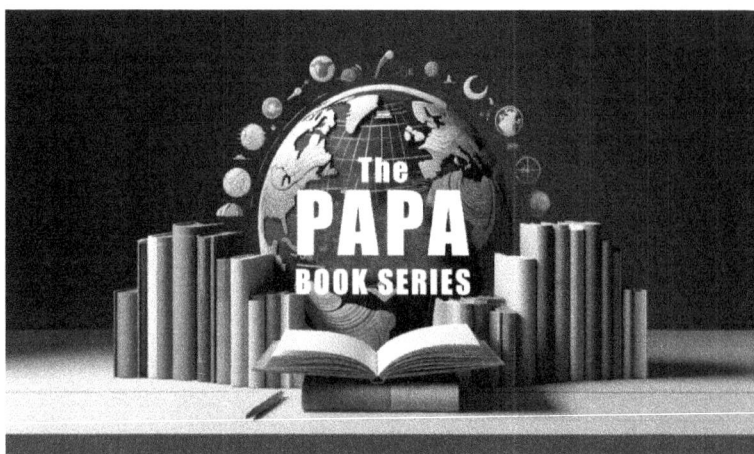

SERIES TITLES AVAILABLE NOW:

(Includes books newly released or publishing soon)

PAPA #1: The Boy in England and Growing Up Tough
is a tale of resilience and survival from
David's early days in England.

PAPA #2: The Young Man in Canada provides a look at
his transformative years in Canada, filled with personal
and professional growth.

**PAPA #3: The Businessman and Entrepreneur in the
USA** chronicles David's entry into the business world
and his entrepreneurial adventures in the United States.

PAPA #4: The Entrepreneur: PAPAS Secret #4 takes a
deep dive into his entrepreneurial mindset and the
lessons learned from building businesses.

PAPA #12: The Famous 50 Book Series is an exciting global vanity publishing project, connecting famous people across industries at *www.famous50.com.*

PAPA #13: GenMar – Generational Marketing Strategy – Basket to Casket Marketing 101 - reveals how understanding generational values can transform marketing and deepen customer connection.

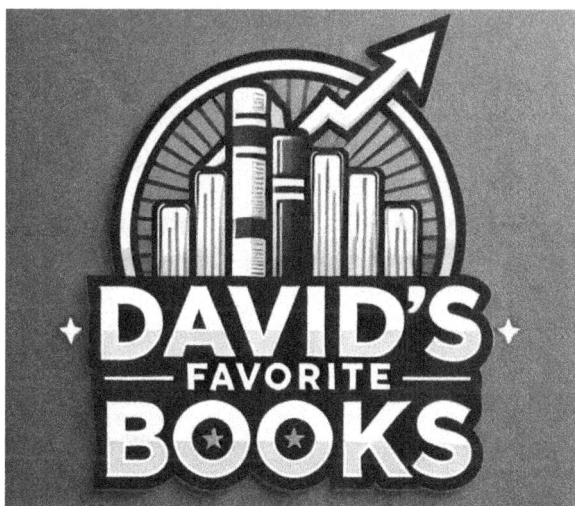

"How to Win Friends and Influence People"
by Dale Carnegie

"The Magic of Thinking Big"
by David J. Schwartz

"Think and Grow Rich"
by Napoleon Hill

"The Power of Positive Thinking"
by Norman Vincent Peale

"The Power of Focus"
by Jack Canfield, Mark Victor Hansen, and Les Hewitt

David's Favorite Books - *Continued*

"The Aladdin Factor"
by Jack Canfield and Mark Victor Hansen

"Innovation and Entrepreneurship"
by Peter F. Drucker

"Secrets of Power Negotiating"
by Roger Dawson

"See You at the Top"
by Zig Ziglar

"Live Your Dreams"
by Les Brown

The Art of Exceptional Living"
by Jim Rohn

The Art of the Deal
Donald J. Trump
45th & 47th President of the United States

**"Maximum Achievement:
Strategies and Skills That Will Unlock
Your Hidden Powers"**
by Brian Tracy

"The 21 Irrefutable Laws of Leadership"
by John C. Maxwell

My Creed

By Dean Alfange

A powerful declaration of
self-reliance, entrepreneurship and personal freedom.

I do not choose to be a common man,
It is my right to be uncommon ... if I can,
I seek opportunity ... not security.
I do not wish to be a kept citizen.
Humbled and dulled by having the
State look after me.
I want to take the calculated risk;
To dream and to build.
To fail and to succeed.
I refuse to barter incentive for a dole;
I prefer the challenges of life
To the guaranteed existence;
The thrill of fulfillment
To the stale calm of Utopia.
I will not trade freedom for beneficence
Nor my dignity for a handout
I will never cower before any master
Nor bend to any threat.
It is my heritage to stand erect.
Proud and unafraid;
To think and act for myself,
To enjoy the benefit of my creations
And to face the world boldly and say:
This, with God's help, I have done.

All this is what it means to be an
"Entrepreneur."

-Acknowledgements-

To the individuals listed below who I have been privileged to meet personally, I would like to publicly say "thank you" for the inspiration I received from meeting you. That inspiration has deeply impacted my life and success.
With appreciation -- David Selley

Robert Allen
Nothing Down Real Estate and Author
I bought his "nothing down" book and just did it. Later on I was grateful to be on his national infomercials and featured in his 2nd Chancers book.
www.robertallen.com

Foster Brooks
I had the pleasure of sharing 3-4 first-class flights with the comic Foster from JFK to LAX. He was genuinely funny and sincere, effortlessly entertaining the first-class cabin with his quick wit. On one occasion, I even picked up his luggage. Great memories!

Acknowledgements – *continued*

Les Brown
Famous Motivational Speaker
We met at a function in Atlanta, and I have been inspired by his words ever since.
www.lesbrown.com

George Carlin
A close neighbor on the island in Westlake Village, CA. George had a challenging intellect and a brilliant mind.

William (Bill) Chaplin
is a beautiful example of a "true" entrepreneur. At the age of 18 he defied traditional customs and pursued his dream. He now builds high performance racing cars experiencing a multitude of class wins and national championship honours. If you need a custom car, contact Bill.
www.empireracingcars.com

Prince Charles, Now King of England
Then Prince Charles was the patron of the Royal Bath & West Show in Somerset England. We met at the VIP tent when celebrating Queen Elizabeth's Silver Jubilee. A treasured and inspirational memory.

Rich DeVos, Founder Amway Corporation
Rich offered to help my family during a critical medical emergency. As profit sharing Direct Distributors, I will never forget his kindness. A truly remarkable man who created opportunity for millions and a great company.
www.amway.com

Acknowledgements– *continued*

Elton Gallegly
Thirteen Term California Congressman
Elton was directly responsible for arranging an emergency medical evacuation for our Veteran son from Germany to Texas. I will be eternally grateful for that!

Deborah Gardner
Mrs. Arizona in 2020 and Mrs. America in 2022
is a renowned entrepreneur, author, professional aquatic swimmer, and keynote motivational speaker. She delivers powerful messages globally.
www.iamdeborahg.com

Steve Harrison
Internationally Acclaimed Media and
Personal Development Expert
Steve's powerful guidance and vast media background are guiding me through the launch of my book series. I am grateful for his wisdom and knowledge.
www.steveharrison.com

Mark Victor Hansen
Co-author - The Chicken Soup Book Series
(500 million copies sold!)
A powerful thought leader and transformational thinker, you have taught me how to focus on meaningful story telling. Plus, I loved being part of your exciting Enlightened Millionaire program.
www.markvictorhansen.com

Acknowledgements – *continued*

Robert Kiyosaki
Your financial wisdom, particularly in
Rich Dad Poor Dad, has shaped my financial strategies.
Thank you for that! - *www.richdad.com*

Carol Lawrence
At 92, this famous and vibrant Broadway star, best
known for her iconic role as Maria in *West Side Story*
and numerous appearances, including seven at the
White House, continues to inspire me. She remains
sharp and down-to-earth despite her polished career.
It has been my pleasure to assist her in many ways and
she continues to inspire me with her wit, charm,
energy and positive attitude.

Ron LeGrand
Real Estate Guru
On a fishing trip to Alaska Ron gave me some great
advice "scratch the barnacles' off your brain and release
yourself to YOUR future. That was a very powerful
message from a guy who knows a lot about real estate.
I appreciate his valuable mentorship!
www.ronlegrand.com

Bob Proctor
Great Thought Leader and
Personal Development Expert
I met Bob at an NSA event in Phoenix. He gave me
one piece of great advice that I will never forget.
"Don't let negativity into your life"
That is wonderful advice for everyone!
www.proctorgallagherinstitute.com

136

Acknowledgements– *continued*

Jim Rohn
Internationally acclaimed Business and Personal Development Speaker

I was on Jim's last call the day before he died from pulmonary respiratory failure. A remarkable man who has helped millions. – *www.jimrohn.com*

Mickey Rooney

Mickey lived a few doors away from us on the island in West Lake Village, California. We often exchanged pleasantries and frequent visits to the pizza parlor.

Donald Trump
President of the United States

I met Donald at a Jeff Kaller event in Orlando. He said one thing to me that has changed my life. "When you come up with an idea, pull the trigger immediately". That is what I do now! He sent my wife and I a beautiful card for our 60th wedding anniversary. A true entrepreneur and patriot!

Bud Westmore

Bud was one of the famous Westmore brothers from Universal Studios, also a devoted Anglophile. His Encino home reflected British charm, complete with a knight in armor. During lunch at his studio, he showed me the Mermaid and Psycho props. His love for England was clear in our long conversations.

Acknowledgements– *continued*

Christian Yelich
Our grandkids and Christian played together at
family parties when we lived in Westlake Village, CA.
Now, a famous MVP and Allstar baseball player.
A true inspiration for me and millions of kids.

*"Though we have not met personally, I want to express
my gratitude to the following individuals for their
insights and wisdom, which have been invaluable to me in
accomplishing this book series. Thank you for sharing
your knowledge with the world."*

Dale Carnegie	John Maxwell
Jack Canfield	Norman Vincent Peale
Peter Drucker	Julia Roberts
Roger Dawson	Tony Robbins
Napoleon Hill	Zig Ziglar

Contact David Selley
through www.*DavidSelley.net*
to obtain information about volume
discounts, The Step-by-Step Coaching
Programs, licensing partnership
opportunities, speaker availability.

Three lives - three countries

Regional - National – International

©2016

International Entrepreneurs Association

We provide global product distribution and entrepreneurial training through our network of Executive Directors worldwide. Though our business model is new, it is rich in experience, offering a fresh, innovative approach to global business. Our world-class team is driven by need, not greed, with a mission to help marginalized entrepreneurs reach their fullest potential. We aim to serve humanity, leaving a legacy of progress, personal growth, and upholding the highest standards of integrity and core values.

Join the IEA
(International Entrepreneurs Association)
Want to build something that lasts—
and grow with like-minded leaders?

www.iea777.com

Senior Parks Project

The U.S. faces a critical shortage of affordable senior housing, and Senior Parks USA aims to address this with a national chain of 100-acre parks featuring small, ergonomically designed manufactured homes for seniors. Over the next decade, the plan is to offer dignified, affordable housing to millions of seniors.

www.seniorparksusa.com

The One Day Event for Seniors
Music, Moods & Memories

The One Day Event hosted by **Long Live Seniors** is a unique, interactive experience designed to enrich the lives of seniors by offering valuable resources, expert guidance, and opportunities to connect with others in their community. Focused on promoting health, wellness, and longevity, this event is a one-stop opportunity for seniors and their families to learn, engage, and be inspired.

Event Overview

The One Day Event offers a full day of workshops, seminars, and activities tailored to the needs and interests of seniors. The event is designed to empower seniors by giving them the tools and knowledge they need to live longer, healthier, and more fulfilling lives.

www.LongLiveSeniors.com

MARR▮ED

David & Sonja
SELLEY

65 Years of Love and Partnership

With over 65 years of marriage, we've discovered that love is a daily decision. Our Married Program provides proven tools to help couples navigate challenges, resolve conflicts, and strengthen their bond. Using the powerful 95-5 and 1-10 techniques, you'll learn how to solve any problem and communicate effectively. Plus, uncover the 10 simple questions that can transform your relationship and deepen your connection. Whether you're rekindling the spark or building a stronger foundation, this program offers a roadmap for lasting love and harmony. Start your journey today and create your own enduring love story.

www.happylifeexpert.com

© 2016

Famous 50 Publishing Series

The Famous 50 Publishing Series offers professionals in over 100 industries the chance to join an exclusive first edition book, featuring 50 top performers. With a 4-page spread for your bio and contact details, this vanity publication is a powerful promotional tool. Gain global exposure and prestige while showcasing your expertise alongside high achievers.

www.famous50.com

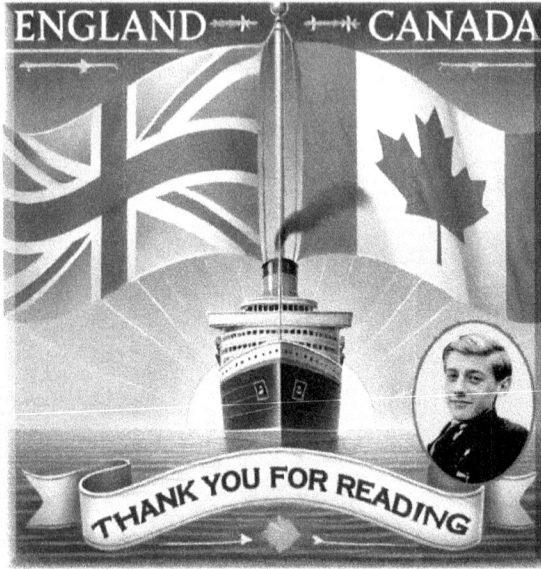

ENGLAND → ← CANADA

THANK YOU FOR READING

If you enjoyed this book, be sure to explore the rest of the *PAPA Book Series*. Each book offers a unique perspective on David's remarkable life and invaluable lessons on entrepreneurship, family, and success. Stay tuned for more inspiring titles to come!

Contact David Selley

www.iea777.com

davidselley08@gmail.com

1-800-388-3102

Coming Soon:

GenMar Toolkit –
Practical Tools for Loyalty,
Relevance & Generational Impact

| ALIGN YOUR MESSAGE | ACROSS GENERATIONS | BUILD CUSTOMER LOYALTY | LEAD WITH EMOTIONAL CLARITY |

You've just explored the core of the GenMar Strategy — a powerful framework for understanding how different generations think, trust, and respond to brand messaging.

And now, we're taking it a step further.

The GenMar Toolkit is the next phase — a practical resource packed with tools, templates, and training to help you implement these generational strategies across your brand, marketing, hiring, and customer experience. Whether you're a solo entrepreneur or leading a team, the Toolkit will help you:

- Identify and close generational trust gaps
- Speak with emotional clarity across age groups

- Build brand loyalty that spans decades
- Train your team to communicate with purpose

Want First Access?
The Toolkit is in final development —
and you're invited to be first in line.

Join the priority list at
www.GenMarStrategy.com/notify

We'll notify you when the Toolkit is released, along with early access to sample tools, live sessions, and opportunities for keynote speaking, workshops, or consulting.

This is more than a marketing system.
It's a generational movement.

www.ingramcontent.com/pod-product-compliance
Lightning Source LLC
Chambersburg PA
CBHW071554200326
41519CB00021BB/6746